"In this beautiful anthology of familiar favorites and new discoveries, Gary Bouchard clearly demonstrates the marvelous intersections between art and belief, art and life. Bouchard not only teaches us to pray; he teaches us to live more deeply through the mystery of faith embodied in language. Never didactic, never pretentious, his sincere and enlightening prefaces and summaries for each poem are like being in the company of a beloved professor or an old friend. This thoughtful collection may be read in a variety of ways, but whatever approach the reader takes, Bouchard and his chosen poets awaken us to the joy and truth at the center of our collective and spiritual being. This is a book to cherish, to teach, and to share."

—David A. King
Professor of English
Kennesaw State University

"Bouchard's whole book is a poem, a psalm, a prayer . . . word becomes WORD. How? Bouchard connects each poem with a good dose of daily life and human yearning that . . . somehow . . . leads to prayer. He invites, nudges, and encourages readers to open a poem by linking it with their own experiences. His book includes a marvelous variety of poets and is like a modern psalmody worthy of praying."

—Thomasita Homan, OSB
Oblate Director at Mount St. Scholastica, Atchison,
Kansas, and professor emerita at Benedictine College

Twenty Poems to Pray

Gary M. Bouchard

LITURGICAL PRESS
Collegeville, Minnesota

www.litpress.org

© 2019 by Gary M. Bouchard
Published by Liturgical Press, Collegeville, Minnesota. All rights reserved. No part of this book may be used or reproduced in any manner whatsoever, except brief quotations in reviews, without written permission of Liturgical Press, Saint John's Abbey, PO Box 7500, Collegeville, MN 56321-7500. Printed in the United States of America.

1   2   3   4   5   6   7   8   9

Library of Congress Cataloging-in-Publication Data

Names: Bouchard, Gary M., 1961– author.
Title: Twenty poems to pray / Gary M. Bouchard.
Description: Collegeville : Liturgical Press, 2019. | Summary: "A resource for reflection and prayer using poetry from several writers"—Provided by publisher.
Identifiers: LCCN 2019014597 (print) | LCCN 2019980350 (ebook) | ISBN 9780814664698 (pbk.) | ISBN 9780814664940 (ebook)
Subjects: LCSH: Religious poetry, American—History and criticism. | Religious poetry, English—History and criticism. | Prayer—Poetry. | Prayer. | Prayer in literature.
Classification: LCC PS310.R4 B68 2019 (print) | LCC PS310.R4 (ebook) | DDC 811/.009382—dc23
LC record available at https://lccn.loc.gov/2019014597
LC ebook record available at https://lccn.loc.gov/2019980350

Prayer (I)

Prayer, the church's banquet, angel's age,
God's breath in man returning to his birth,
The soul in paraphrase, heart in pilgrimage,
The Christian plummet sounding heav'n and earth
Engine against th' Almighty, sinner's tow'r,
Reversed thunder, Christ-side-piercing spear,
The six-days world transposing in an hour,
A kind of tune, which all things hear and fear;
Softness, and peace, and joy, and love, and bliss,
Exalted manna, gladness of the best,
Heaven in ordinary, man well drest,
The milky way, the bird of Paradise,
Church-bells beyond the stars heard, the soul's blood,
The land of spices; something understood.

—*George Herbert*

Contents

Introduction

Poetry and prayer are close cousins, if not siblings. We can be certain, I think, that long before David took up his lyre to intone his psalms of protest, penance, and praise to the Hebrew God, the human breath that first gave shape to words had already knitted together these two oral expressions. The longings of those of us who yearn to know and feel and express our connection with the divine are, like the winged horse-sense of Pegasus, always trying with the unsteady wings of words to ascend upward.

It's true that most poetry is not prayer and that many prayers make for pretty mediocre poetry, but both the earnest petitioner and the determined poet may each be said to achieve their highest aim when they deploy language with such grace and inspiration that their expressions transcend language itself. Sometimes, as with most of the selections in this volume, poems are prayers. In the case of other poems offered here, they contain a longing of a kind that allows them to serve as a sort of prayer.

Before proceeding in an attempt to derive earnest prayer from poems, though, it seems reasonable to have some agreement upon what is meant by "a sort of prayer." And given the nature of this small book, what better way to do so than in a poem?

The reluctant seventeenth-century Anglican priest, George Herbert, consciously made all of his poems prayers, and many of them, like the one included in the fifth section of this book are astonishing. In a remarkable poem entitled simply "Prayer," which I have placed as this book's epigraph, Herbert—without explanation, commentary, or argument— artfully assembles in English sonnet form what amounts to a list of twenty-seven metaphorical descriptions of what prayer is and what prayer does. To best appreciate the range and power of the descriptions he offers us, I forsake, with some reluctance, the intricately rhymed construction of the poet's fourteen lines, and simply list here in order of occurrence the possibilities he provides:

1. the church's banquet
2. angel's age
3. God's breath in man returning to his birth
4. the soul in paraphrase
5. heart in pilgrimage
6. the Christian plummet sounding heav'n and earth
7. engine against th' Almighty
8. sinner's tow'r
9. reversed thunder
10. Christ-side-piercing spear
11. the six-days world transposing in an hour
12. a kind of tune, which all things hear and fear
13. softness
14. peace
15. joy
16. love
17. bliss
18. exalted manna
19. gladness at the best
20. heaven in ordinary
21. man well-dressed
22. the milky way

23. the bird of Paradise
24. Church-bells beyond the stars heard
25. the soul's blood
26. the land of spices
27. something understood

A few of these descriptions are certainly predictable, and others may be somewhat parochial. But most are provocative, and a few are, to my mind, just plain combustible. Some people, I suppose, might want to remove a few of Herbert's descriptions from the list or add one or two of their own. My aim in providing it is not to hold it up for its orthodox theological correctness, nor to engender an academic or any other kind of debate about the nature of prayer, of which I am, at best, a practiced amateur.

I offer this list simply as a reasonable and inspiring invitation to prayer. If one or more of the twenty-seven resonates with you, pocket it and proceed forward into the pages ahead.

The endeavor of this small book is not to offer analysis, but to prompt meditation. I have tried to offer just enough words of my own by way of explanation and context to help readers apprehend, appreciate, reflect upon, and ultimately somehow pray these poets' verses on their own.

I invite and encourage you in the pages and seasons ahead to use the words of poets as vehicles to express "heaven in ordinary" or to praise like "exalted manna"; to find the right "paraphrase" for your own soul or maybe sense your "soul's blood"; to muster up from your grief or anger "reversed thunder" or dare to articulate from your own personal anguish "Christ-side-piercing spear." To voice "something understood." If peace, joy, love, or bliss are engendered in any form or quantity for any reader, then my effort has been more than worth its while.

Part I

When Yellow Leaves
or None or Few

Pied Beauty

Fr. Gerard Manley Hopkins, SJ (1844–1889)

It would be hard to find a more universal prayer than the simple, laudatory declaratives: "Glory be to God . . . Praise him."

These are the first and last words of a poem that speaks with all of the earnestness of a child beholding the wonders of God's creation for the first time. The nine lines of verse in between these two familiar declaratives, though playful in their childlike expressions, are as extravagant in their auditory, visual, and tactile imagery, and as intricate in their poetic construction as any passage of verse from the Psalms.

The first poem I offer here to pray is the work of England's most famous modern Catholic poet, Gerard Manley Hopkins, SJ. It is helpful to those unacquainted with Fr. Hopkins, and prudent for those who are, to qualify those four descriptors of his person. He was certainly *English*, as English as his Oxford pedigree and the Victorian bowler and muttonchops he sported in early photographs. *Fame* was something he certainly did not know during his short and often lonely life, and *modern* is a designation that would only make sense decades later when critics began to perceive how his ingenious experimentations with form and syntax and meter—like those of Emily Dickinson and Walt Whitman on the American continent—anticipated so much of the poetry that came after him in the twentieth century. *Roman Catholic* was something Hopkins became by conversion under the guidance of Bl. Cardinal John Henry Newman during the Oxford movement.

And as though being an English Catholic did not estrange him enough from his family and his proper Victorian upbringing, Gerard took the further step of joining what he and others perceived to be the most severe religious order, and eventually was ordained a Jesuit priest. This vocation, to which he remained unflaggingly faithful, was an unlikely and clumsy path for an aspiring poet, and especially one with the eccentricities that accompany an especially keen sensitivity to and admiration of the natural world.

Finding him kneeling on a walkway studying insects or rapt in meditation as he stared in the sky admiring a bird's flight, his superiors would seek a more suitable assignment for him. When, in a homily at the Farm Street Church in London's dowdy Mayfair district, the young Hopkins shocked the pious ladies by comparing the extravagant love of God to the abundant milk from a cow's udders, he was quickly transferred again so that he would come to refer to himself as "fortune's football."

A scholar of classical languages, Hopkins would eventually find himself assigned to teach Greek at University College Dublin, the Catholic alternative to Trinity that Cardinal Newman had founded on St. Stephen's Green. There he contracted typhoid fever and died at the age of forty-four, after which his Jesuit colleagues burned his belongings—including all of his papers—after burying him in a collective anonymous grave in Dublin's suburbs.

The final years of Hopkins's life in Dublin have always been perceived as ones of despondency because of his perceived exile from his family and his beloved England, and because of the so-called dark sonnets he wrote during those years. But a recent and important corrective by the contemporary poet and critic Desmond Egan called "Hopeful Hopkins" illustrates the humor and levity that marked much of Hopkins's time in Dublin.

Hopeful Hopkins, the poet of such masterpieces as "God's Grandeur" and "As Kingfishers Catch Fire," is the poet whose words you are invited to pray here in a poem called simply and descriptively "Pied Beauty." Before I offer any words of explanation or guidance that may infect your experience of this poem, I urge you to imagine yourself as a child of six or eight years old, find a place where you can be uninterrupted and without any restraint or embarrassment, just pray the words:

Pied Beauty

Glory be to God for dappled things—
For skies of couple-colour as a brinded cow;
For rose-moles all in stipple upon trout that swim;
Fresh-firecoal chestnut-falls; finches' wings;
Landscape plotted and pieced—fold, fallow, and
    plough;
And all trades, their gear and tackle and trim.

All things counter, original, spare, strange;
Whatever is fickle, freckled (who knows how?)
With swift, slow; sweet, sour; adazzle, dim;
He fathers-forth whose beauty is past change.
Praise him.[1]

Amen. As purely fun as these words are to speak, there are words here that our eight-year-old selves may not apprehend at first speaking. "Pied" seems to suggest piety, but in fact it means is multicolored, preparing us for "dappled," spotted; "brinded," patchy colored; and "rose moles all in stipple," which may be read as red dots painted on. "Fresh-firecoal chestnut-falls"—an expression typical of the compound nouns, adjectives, and verbs that Hopkins loved to construct—can be understood by anyone fortunate enough to have seen an abundance of fresh-fallen chestnuts beneath a tree and willing to share Hopkins' notion that they resemble coals in a fire. "Fallow" is ploughed but unsown earth and "adazzle" is an "invented" adjective of Hopkins that is, well, self-explanatory.

So the poet would have us see, with him, a variety of speckled and spotted things in nature, starting with the way clouds resemble the spots on cows, then red-spotted trout, fallen chestnuts, the wings of finches, and the turned-up earth itself. He then has us meditate briefly on the strangeness and dazzling pleasure of it all, embedding as he does so the questions that we often ask ourselves when looking at bright fall foliage, a striking sunset, an ocean scape, or the intricately "painted" back of a small insect: How? Who?

Evolutionary science offers one answer and Hopkins was living when Darwin's natural selection was electric in the air of England. The poet-priest, however, opts for divine selection in a brilliant compound verb comprised of the two most important words in the poem before the final two: "fathers-forth." The grand cloud shapes and tiny dots on fish and finches are "fathered-forth" by the extravagant affection of one whose beauty is constant and unchangeable.

There is for Hopkins but one possible response to this recognition, and his own awe abruptly interrupts his own rhyming pattern in order to make this response. The rhyme scheme of the first stanza is abc, abc. The second stanza starts repeating this pattern with a small variation: dbc. Then, the second "d" ("change") is interrupted when the speaker leaps beyond the expected "b" right to "c" in a truncated final line that springs forth, in almost breathless, near-speechless words we did not hear coming: "Praise him." He thus stops, not ends, where he began.

Now, with perhaps a clearer understanding and appreciation of the effusive invitation to prayer that Fr. Hopkins offers us, go back and pray the words again—out loud and out louder!—with even greater surety and enthusiasm.

If you have prayed this prayer aloud you have felt the poet's expressions on your tongue and tonsils. Hopkins has tickled your lips and made them smile. May this smile be our very own prayer of gratitude for our very own plotted and still uncultivated lives. And as one more act of praise, I encourage you, if you can, to find a child to whom you can speak these speckled words of Fr. Hopkins. In her face, and in the speckled landscape about you, and in fallen chestnuts and cracked acorns of autumn, may you see and hear this poem again, and pray it often with hopeful Fr. Hopkins.

September, the First Day of School

Howard Nemerov (1920–1991)

Surely I was not the only one to feel a pit of trepidation in my stomach upon seeing in early August a giant banner announcing BACK-TO-SCHOOL SALE! Summoned from our summer reverie into rows of school desks, many of us understood Huck Finn's worries. They were trying to civilize us. My wife, who has an early August birthday, recalls the arrival of her birthday as an unwelcome harbinger that summer was about to come to an end. And as we have spent our lives together as educators in New Hampshire, we have grown ever conscious of summer's brevity and the return to longer days of work and shorter days of daylight that the surprising chill of late summer nights portends.

This made us sympathetic parents to our two free-range sons when they were beckoned by September to forego sun-drenched days of lake water in the ears, saltwater up the nose, scraped knees, and postponed bedtimes on hot nights lit with the falling embers of fireworks. What we knew as they dragged summer's last lunker from the lake, however, is something they have still yet to appreciate: each September, and especially the first, was a time of heart-wrenching letting go.

When asked to name my favorite poem, Howard Nemerov's "September, the First Day of School" always rises near the top. No other poem I know speaks more eloquently to the enormous faith it takes to raise a child. And whether one is a parent or not, its words are a powerful and assuring reflection on the surrender we all must make to the many things that lie beyond our control. I have read this poem on many public occasions and given it to friends when their children crossed that ominous threshold of first grade for the first time. It is a poem that has engendered its share of tears, my own, I admit, among them. The final of the six stanzas is a stirring and earnest prayer, and I have learned over time to pray all of the stanzas that precede it. I can recommend that you try to do the same.

The poem is the work of a great twentieth-century American poet, Howard Nemerov, who was twice named America's poet laureate. The son of Russian Jewish immigrants, he was raised in New York City where his father owned a popular department store. After attending Harvard, Nemerov served in World War II as a pilot in both the Royal Canadian Air Force and the U.S. Army Air Forces. Immediately after the war he published his first book of poetry and began teaching at several New England colleges until 1969 when he accepted an appointment as Professor of English and Distinguished Poet in Residence at Washington University in St. Louis where he stayed until his death in 1991. I was fortunate to meet Mr. Nemerov once and hear him read his poetry soon after his *Collected Poems* (1977) was published and awarded a remarkable triple crown: the National Book Award for Poetry, the Pulitzer Prize for Poetry, and the Bollingen Prize.

"September, the First Day of School" begins with a father's description of bringing his son to school for the first time and watching him "disappear behind the schoolroom door." The event prompts him to recall how he "cried at that door a life ago" when he "may have had a hard time letting go." As we all did, and still do. The poet's reflections invoke from Scripture "the dreaming of a little boy" named Joseph that "got him such hatred of his brothers / As cost the greater part of life to mend." As the parent contemplates the unknown future that lies in front of his child, the poem's two parts each end with the beautiful refrain that is its earnest prayer.

Whether you are a parent or child or both, ready your own memories. Recall with Howard Nemerov that first September of letting go. You need not check your tears in order to pray as every parent has:

September, the First Day of School

My child and I hold hands on the way to school,
And when I leave him at the first-grade door
He cries a little but is brave; he does
Let go. My selfish tears remind me how
I cried before that door a life ago.
I may have had a hard time letting go.

Each fall the children must endure together
What every child also endures alone:
Learning the alphabet, the integers,
Three dozen bits and pieces of a stuff
So arbitrary, so peremptory,
That worlds invisible and visible

Bow down before it, as in Joseph's dream
The sheaves bowed down and then the stars bowed
    down
Before the dreaming of a little boy.
That dream got him such hatred of his brothers
As cost the greater part of life to mend,
And yet great kindness came of it in the end.

II

A school is where they grind the grain of thought,
And grind the children who must mind the thought.
It may be those two grindings are but one,
As from the alphabet come Shakespeare's Plays,
As from the integers comes Euler's Law,
As from the whole, inseparably, the lives,

The shrunken lives that have not been set free
By law or by poetic phantasy.
But may they be. My child has disappeared
Behind the schoolroom door. And should I live
To see his coming forth, a life away,
I know my hope, but do not know its form

Nor hope to know it. May the fathers he finds
Among his teachers have a care of him
More than his father could. How that will look
I do not know, I do not need to know.
Even our tears belong to ritual.
But may great kindness come of it in the end.[2]

That children and their thoughts will be grinded in school
is sobering, and surely part of the fear every parent feels while
watching their children pass over the threshold into formal
education. We remain our children's first teachers, it is true,
but we must also let them go into the world to discover for
themselves how integers work, what language can do, what
really happened in history, and why they believe what they do
about life. We want them and their lives to be "set free" by
what they learn, but we also fear that freedom above all else.

   This is work in which I am privileged to participate every
day of my working life, and always with the empathy of a

parent, mindful of the risks and responsibility, the worry and the wonder that justifies the tears at the first-grade door as well as those at college freshmen orientation. For, home-school if we choose, helicopter if we feel we must, we can still only control so much as the world opens up before our growing children.

This is where the praying begins in earnest: may the fathers and mothers our children find among their teachers, coaches, and mentors not just keep them safe and impart good knowledge, but "have a care for them" that fills in the inevitable gaps of our own shortcomings as their primary teachers.

And if we are blessed to see our children "coming forth, a life away," we know what we hope for them "but do not know its form." Young Joseph's father could not have imagined the destiny that awaited his daydreaming youngest son with the colorful coat. And Jesus' parents, who feared in distress that they had lost their only son before discovering him teaching behind the temple doors, most certainly would not have willed upon him the suffering he would endure. "And yet great kindness came of it in the end."

The chronic worry of every parent arises from the fact that we "do not know." The assurance that comes with faith is that we "do not need to know." We struggle to surrender. We seek the grace to trust, and, joining our worried hands with those of Mary and Joseph and all the parents that have come before us—including our own—we do . . . "let go," praying fervently as we do: *May great kindness come of it in the end.*

Sonnet 73

William Shakespeare (1564–1616)

Praying Shakespeare? While the great English bard shaped our understanding of human nature more than any other writer, even those of us who admire his plays and poems the most may find it a stretch to hear or voice his words as intonations to the divine. But if we allow Herbert's "heart in pilgrimage" and "a kind of tune, which all things hear and fear" to guide us, at least one of Shakespeare's 154 sonnets can serve as a stirring spiritual entreaty. The poem, "Sonnet 73," is as close to a perfect lyrical poem as any other I have read. It contains, in three increasingly somber stanzas, the beckoning of the medieval emblem *memento mori*: remember death.

That Shakespeare was a secret Roman Catholic is an idea that has moved over the past several decades from a spurious fringe notion to a seriously regarded aspect of this author's life. He lived in a time and place of dangerous Catholic-Protestant conflict and bore witness to the treacherous conspiracies and atrocities of his age. Whether he was merely a sympathizer to England's old faith, having been raised in a covertly Catholic family in a very Catholic district of England, or whether he risked being a more entangled supporter or even private practitioner of Catholicism we may never know for certain, but excellent scholarship continues to enlighten our understanding of the troublesome choices faced by people of all religious dispositions in the Tudor and Jacobean worlds.

Though the sonnet I offer here contains one very poignant expression of the poet's Catholic sympathies, the circumstance it depicts and the prayer it provokes are decidedly universal. Keeping with the poetic fashion of his day, Shakespeare wrote a cycle of sonnets during the 1590s that were not published until 1609. The poems, which taken together do not form a very cohesive plot, feature an older man praising a younger man's youth and beauty and urging him to get married and have children so that his beauty might endure. On the surface this strikes us as a very uninteresting conversation to be listening in on. Even as the speaker starts to complain about some great injustice he has suffered ("When in disgrace with fortune and men's eyes" [29]), and turns to describing the lovers' triangle in which he and the young man are apparently entangled ("That thou hast her it is not all my grief" [42]), we may wish to stand at a safe distance from these private preoccupations.

For the most genuinely curious readers of Shakespeare's sonnets, the cryptic, self-revelatory bits of gossip they seem to contain are actually the least interesting aspects of the poems. These poems have lived for four centuries beyond the murky sixteenth-century human conflicts they record because they unfold in intricate and provocative layers of metaphor and imagery our three central human preoccupations and predicaments: *love, death,* and *time.* That these private meditations live within the demanding confines of the English sonnet form make their transcendence across four centuries all the more astounding. For over thirty years I have led a public reading of Shakespeare's sonnets on the April day that marks both his birth and death, and I am continually surprised how quickly and fervently some unsuspecting readers personalize the sonnet they are assigned.

In "Sonnet 73" the speaker describes not the young man's aging, but his own. So, contemplate as you speak these words your own accumulation of years and memory. Take a breath before you read, and feel free to sigh as you go:

Sonnet 73

That time of year thou mayst in me behold
When yellow leaves, or none, or few, do hang
Upon those boughs which shake against the cold,
Bare ruin'd choirs, where late the sweet birds sang.
In me thou see'st the twilight of such day,
As after sunset fadeth in the west,
Which by-and-by black night doth take away,
Death's second self, that seals up all in rest.
In me thou see'st the glowing of such fire
That on the ashes of his youth doth lie,
As the death-bed whereon it must expire
Consum'd with that which it was nourish'd by.
    This thou perceivest, which makes thy love more
       strong,
    To love that well which thou must leave ere long.[3]

To apprehend more than just the lovely language, you will of course need to read these lines again. And again. It is time well spent. Note as you reread that the poem is in four parts. There are three separately rhymed quatrains of abab, cdcd, efef that culminate in the final couplet of gg. Each quatrain contains a separate and intricately developed image that leads to the poem's resolution.

Here, before you read again, is a simple summary:

Quatrain 1 ("That time of year thou may'st . . ."): "You look at my face and see the fading leaves on the trees."

Quatrain 2 ("In me thou see'st the twilight . . . "): "You look at me and see the dusk at the end of the day."

Quatrain 3 ("In me thou see'st the glowing . . . "): "You look at me and see the last smoldering coals of a dying fire."

Couplet ("this thou perceives . . . "): "You notice how old I am getting and it makes you love me even more now that you are leaving me."

Now, with this clarification of the meaning, speak the poem again, imagining as you do that you are speaking to your spouse, your child, your grandchild, or a dear friend as they are about to leave you.

The poem's emotional resonance grows with each reading. *Memento mori*, remembering death, is something that the vast majority of people today would regard as merely morbid, but Shakespeare and the generations of humanity who have preceded us considered the daily recognition of our mortality to be the beginning of wisdom.

This poem's beauty is compounded by the several thought treasures it contains. For example, note that in the first quatrain the leaves may be "yellow" (peak foliage), "few" (mid-November), or "none" (autumn over and winter arrived). How old is the person speaking? How old is that person to whom you are saying goodbye in your own life? It may depend upon the light in the room, the fondness of your shared memories, or the size of your worries.

In this same quatrain, Shakespeare makes what for him would have been a dangerous allusion, when the aging speaker compares the bare branches of the trees to "bare ruined choirs, where late the sweet birds sang." The young Shakespeare grew up in a landscape populated with former Catholic abbeys that had been confiscated by King Henry

VIII decades earlier. Most of those abbeys, and the choir stalls where the now exiled monks once sang, had become bare and ruined by Shakespeare's day. Looking at autumn's bare branches, from where the birds have now fled, the poet recalls the emptied abbeys where prayers were once sung, and casually places the silent prayer benches in his poem about aging and loss.

And notice that in the second quatrain we are not seeing a sunset, but the moment after the sun is vanished; a time when there is still some light in the sky, but when the cooling air alerts us to the rapid onset of darkness and when we know how quickly sleep, or "death's second-self" might be upon us. Then in the dying fire of the third quatrain we are offered the profound paradox of our physical existence. The same wood that fuels a fire becomes the ashes that choke it off. Just so, in illness and aging, we are all consumed by the very things that once nourished us. The intricate parts of our flesh that sustained us will eventually be our undoing. The hips and knees that made us run become our daily aches. The heart that kept us living so long becomes a source of worry as it weakens. These are worries we and other perceive. Dwelling upon them may be but a source of regret and grousing. But to those who embrace the hope and promise of the resurrection, each ache and each farewell is but another opportunity for the wisdom urged upon people every Ash Wednesday when they have the ashes described in this poem smudged upon their brows.

When is any meaningful parting in our lives not a kind of prayer? Especially if it is a leave-taking accompanied by illness or evident aging. All of our hearts are in pilgrimage and none of us ever knows when we will see the ones we love again. The greater the distance of time or travel between us, the more this is true. Acceptance of the fact that our lives will fade or are fading—like the leaves on the trees, like the light at the end of the day, like diminished flames—should deepen our gratitude for the great gift that is our life. As autumn's colors fade and daylight shrinks to increasing darkness, many of us look to Advent's hope that we will learn to live in habitual gratitude, and "love more well" the people and the gifts that we must "leave ere long."

Part II
A Small Thing Always Near

Hope

Emily Dickinson (1830–1886)
Kevin Hadduck (b. 1957)

When everything else has been lost, we are assured by St. Paul that three things remain: *faith, hope,* and *love.* The greatest of these, he insists, is love (1 Corinthians 13:13), and who would argue with that? Asked to choose the second enduring virtue most of us would likely choose faith, leaving hope a delicate and oft-neglected third, sitting quietly in the middle of this trio of spiritual treasures.

Consider how we speak about hope. We hope for better days ahead. We pin our hopes on things. We say that hope springs eternal, which more often than not expresses a sort of ironic skepticism about the gap between one's aspirations and what our experience suggests will actually happen. Even our frequent use of the word hopefully, which must have been originally constructed to mean "full of hope," now usually signals our doubt and worry.

To actually be filled with hope, most of us learned from a young age, can lead to crushing disappointment. So as we grow older, we tend to hedge our bets by playing the game of low expectations. "Well," we say, "here's hoping," but the concern in our hearts is revealed in the tone of our voice which indicates just how precariously hope abides in our lives. Every prayer, it seems to me, is nothing if not an expression of hope. And since despair is the complete absence of hope, it seems that even our most desperate prayers, by being voiced or being thought or felt, are some expression of hope.

Nearly two hundred years ago Emily Dickinson, the astounding poet—who for all her purported reclusiveness was more awake than most people during the Great Awakening that engulfed her quiet town of Amherst, Massachusetts—made the fragile but constant assurances of hope tangible in the body of a small bird:

314

"Hope" is the thing with feathers -
That perches in the soul -
And sings the tune without the words -
And never stops - at all -

And sweetest - in the Gale - is heard
And sore must be the storm -
That could abash the little Bird
That kept so many warm -

I've heard it in the chillest land -
And on the strangest Sea -
But - never - in Extremity -
It asked a crumb - of me.[1]

The characteristically simple alternating rhymes and rhythmic 4-3 ballad beats of this poem make it easy to learn by heart. And while its musical qualities appeal to young children, its words should resonate with all of us who have known "extremity" and the kinds of chilling and strange storms that can "abash" our hopes. When we find ourselves at a loss for how to pray or what to pray, because of one of life's unexpected storms, or just because of the vague, everyday hollowness that can come upon us for any number of reasons, we may at least imagine a little bird perched in our soul, singing a tune that has no words. And not stopping, even though we have. We can, in our extremity, let hope do the praying for us.

Emily Dickinson's poem was recently given new life in the words of a contemporary poet, Kevin Hadduck, who I came to know when he became a teacher and mentor to my youngest son. Kevin engages readers with his reverence for the vast landscapes of his home state of Montana as well as his depiction of the very ordinary circumstances of our clumsy human lives.

Kevin's poems make a subtle but persistent case for faith, hope, and love even as they depict with sometimes painful honesty the mixed success that he, like all of us, has known in living out those fragile and abiding virtues. In his collection of poems *Hymnody of the Blue Heron*, he takes up Emily Dickinson's fragile and wounded bird and brings it to those who need it most desperately. In one way or another, we have all been here:

Hope

Three phone calls:
A farm wife with chest pains
Stealing her breath.
A woman with five children,
Her husband gone with her money.
A man who fears his own mind,
For whom his own thoughts
And hands are strangers.

So here I come,
With a twittering gift from God,
Like a schoolboy
Bringing home a robin
Torn by a cat or a passing car.
They act grateful for this,
Put their hands gingerly
To the frail, demanding body,
To the beak constantly open,
The claws grasping at a finger,
The discomposed feathers
Of a small thing always near
Dying. I say to them, "Here,
Feed it with water and bread."[2]

What happens when people reach out to us from their despair? We are all familiar with the great Prayer of St. Francis. Most of us have let the words "where there is despair let me bring hope" pass over our lips perhaps hundreds of times. But most of us spend our lives avoiding despair at all costs. We carefully step away from where it hunches on city sidewalks. We leave it securely behind the walls of prisons and mental health institutions. We behold it in the addiction-plagued lives that populate the newspapers and evening news. We see it, shake our heads, and turn away.

But then sometimes the phone rings. We receive a troubling email. A neighbor or work colleague unexpectedly reaches out to us in desperate need of hope: a frightening medical diagnosis, a suddenly fractured relationship or family, the early onset of dementia, a job loss, a financial crisis, a sudden death, or just plain old despondency or unyielding depression. Just as St. Augustine famously prayed, "Lord make me chaste, but not yet," we are tempted from our busy lives to pray, "Where there is despair let me bring hope, *but not now!*"

We feel unqualified, inadequate, inconvenienced. We have problems of our own. Who are we to offer hope? We barely have enough of our own. Besides, what can we possibly do or say? Aren't there experts for this kind of thing? But of course if it were easy to bring hope where there is despair St. Francis would not have had to pray for that strength and encourage us to do the same.

These poems by Emily Dickinson and Kevin Hadduck can help us pray St. Francis's prayer in earnest by understanding better the gift we are being asked to bring. When we bring hope to someone in despair, we do not necessarily have to bear the steady, immoveable rock of faith for them to stand upon, or offer them the perfection of unconditional love. The pious assurance of faith may in fact be off-putting and our love may be something that they are not ready to receive.

But hope—well that is "a twittering gift from God" that we can try to carry "like a schoolboy / Bringing home a robin / Torn by a cat or a passing car." Hope knows injury. It has all the fragility of a newborn babe lying in a feeding trough in a borrowed barn on a winter night as the uprooted parents try to keep it safe and ponder their uncertain future. Hope hangs broken, bleeding, and forsaken on a cross, barely able to breathe and feeling forsaken.

Perhaps it isn't as great as love or faith, but we know that sometimes hope is all we seem to have, and when we feel like we don't even have that, we rely on people who, even in clumsy platitudes like "hang in there" or "things will work out in the end" can bring some fragile hope, put its "frail, demanding body" in our hands, and who can lift us beyond our own discouragement and hopelessness with "a small thing" with "discomposed feathers" that is "always near / Dying."

In bringing the gift of hope to someone, we are really just acknowledging their hurt and worry and offering from our own human frailty some small gift of assurance that we pray can be nursed into life. "Here," we say "Feed it with water and bread." We do not walk away feeling heroic, or even assured that we have fixed anything. But where there's despair, we have, from our own awkward inadequacy and bungling brokenness, at least brought "the thing with feathers" that "kept so many warm"—and we *hope* that with some care, and with some prayer, it will sing in our soul and in the souls of others once again.

Stray Moments

William Stafford (1914–1993)

One problem with words is that like other wonderful things in our lives they grow tired with use. This is as true for sacred language as it is for everyday speech. One unintended consequence of the hourly or daily or weekly repetition of familiar prayers is that such routine can inadvertently empty words of their meaning. "[T]hrough my fault, through my fault, / through my most grievous fault." Really? Do we mean that or are they words habitually spilling out of us on liturgical cue?

One thing poets can do for us then is breathe new life into old words and worn-out expressions. They do this by lifting the words from their familiar context and placing them somewhere new. During a spring-cleaning or a move, have you ever seen a familiar piece of furniture out on the lawn? It's like noticing it for the first time. Have you ever loaned a favorite necktie or sweater to someone and seeing it on them remembered why you chose it from the rack in the store in the first place? Well, that's what can happen when an insightful writer lifts familiar language from its usual place. We may see and hear the words and behold their value again for the first time.

William Stafford's poem "Stray Moments" is all about re-appreciation of what is familiar and good and true in our abundantly blessed daily lives. The three sacred words he translates into the poem below are three of the most powerful and frequently spoken in the language, words that too many of us let fall off out of our mouths lifelessly hundreds of times a year: "our daily bread."

But before we see the new life he breathes into these three familiar words, let's learn a bit about Mr. Stafford who died in 1993 after a long life of daily writing and reflection. William Stafford was born in Hutchison, Kansas, in 1914 and grew up in Kansas small towns amid a landscape that instilled a capacity for quiet and humble listening, and with parents who valued language and reverence for the place of God in our lives. A resolute pacifist, Stafford was a conscientious objector during World War II, serving instead in the Conservation Corps. He would eventually earn two degrees from the University of Kansas and a doctorate from the University of Iowa and settle down into a vocation of writing and teaching, mostly at Lewis & Clark College in Oregon, where he would serve for decades as Oregon's poet laureate.

Stafford's first book of published poems didn't come out until he was forty-six, and the title poem "Traveling Through the Dark" about the night traveler who comes upon a dead doe in the road and, before rolling her over the edge, has to come to terms with the still living fawn inside her, placed Stafford on the literary map. The book won the National Book Award for Poetry in 1963 and he would go on to publish fifty-seven volumes of poems, writing every morning of his life, including the day he died. That morning he drafted his last poem, "Are you Mr. William Stafford?" which contains the lines: " 'You don't have to / prove anything,' my mother said. 'Just be ready / for what God sends.' "[3] Stafford died of a heart attack that afternoon.

I remember in college when William Stafford returned to Kansas to read for us. At dinner before the reading he was offered the opportunity to say grace, an honor I am sure he had not anticipated. He said that since he came from the Quaker tradition, he would simply invite us into a moment of silent gratitude. Such calm diplomacy on the spot in a room full of Catholics!

William Stafford has been inviting me into quiet moments ever since. Like this one:

Stray Moments

We used to ask—remember? We said,
". . . our daily bread." And it came.
Now we want more, and security too;
"You can't be too sure." And,
"Why should we trust?—Who says?"
And Old-Who doesn't speak any more.

They used to have Thunder talk, or
The Rivers or Leaves, or Birds. It's all
"Cheep, cheep" now. It's a long time
since a cloud said anything helpful.
But last night a prophet was talking,
disguised as a clerk at the check-out stand:

"Gee, it's been a good day!"
And we talked for awhile and I felt
that I wasn't such a bad guy.
We stood there looking out at the evening.
And maybe what we said, in its way, was
Thanks for our daily bread.[4]

Anyone with even the vaguest acquaintance with the Christian tradition knows the words to the Our Father. When you pray, Jesus, instructed his disciples, pray like this. And we have ever since. Or at least we have repeated the words thousands of times. But wait, Stafford challenges us, "remember?" we asked for our daily bread, "And it came." We got what we asked for. Do we remember that? Are we grateful? Of course not. "Now we want more, and security too." We need equity in our property, cash in the bank, abundance in our retirement and various insurances and passwords and security codes to protect it all because "Who says?" Meanwhile, we mumble reflexively, "Give us this day our daily bread" and when it arrives fresh-baked and whole wheat or to our gluten-free specifications, we eat it, disregard the twelve baskets left over and still worry that there won't be enough because one never knows, better safe than sorry, "You can't be too sure."

Such habitual lack of faith, Stafford suggests leads to "Old-Who"—God I think he means—not speaking anymore. Or at least not being heard by those who will not listen, those to whom he continues to give abundant daily bread without receiving a hint of gratitude.

In the middle stanza of the poem the poet recalls the ancient and archetypal relationship between humanity and the divine, and there is something I think of the vast open landscape of Stafford's Kansas upbringing in these lines. People used to acknowledge with humility that, in Gerard Manley Hopkins's words, "the world is charged with the grandeur of God,"[5] but today the thunder, rivers, leaves, and birds are as unappreciated as the daily bread and other abundances that come our way. "Cheep, cheep" the merchants chirp and we rush in for the sale.

Who can shake us from such shallow and dire complacency? "A prophet." But in our world today it will not be one with wild hair and eyes shouting in the desert: "Repent, for the kingdom of heaven is at hand" (Matt 3:2). No, the prophets we need to heed are like the one in Stafford's poem, "disguised as a clerk at the check-out stand" who said simply, "Gee, it's been a good day!" This prophet, a person of little power, affluence, or authority, is one who simply acknowledged with gratitude the simple goodness that had come his way that day. He took time to talk to the poet-customer, leaving him feeling "that I wasn't such a bad guy." The two of them then "stood there looking out at the evening. / And maybe," he suggests what they said "in its way, was / Thanks for our daily bread."

The simplest of prayers. The simplest of prophesies. May our thoughts and tasks and conversations flow from gratitude for our daily bread—for what has been given us this day. Remember?

The Song Opens

Fr. Karol Wojtyla—St. Pope John Paul II (1920–2005)

Imagine praying the words of the young mother of Jesus as rendered by a poet calling himself a dirt clod. Now imagine that dirt clod seated on the chair of St. Peter!

When Cardinal Karol Wojtyla became Pope John Paul II forty years ago, the world was in for many surprises. One of those surprises might still be startling to many people today, who don't know that the Polish native and now canonized saint was a prolific poet.

A lover of the arts and an actor in Poland's underground theatre, Karol began writing poems in his native Polish when he was a seminarian, completing a stirring sequence entitled *Song of the Hidden God*. As a priest in the 1950s and 1960s, Fr. Wojtyla published his poems in Catholic publications under the pen name "Andrzej Jasień." Andrzej's actual identity was carefully concealed by editors to confound communist censors and prevent Wojtyla from being arrested like many of his fellow priests at a time when the Soviet government sought to squash religious practice. And yes, occasionally the man who would one day become one of the most admired and influential people in recent history published poems under the pseudonym "Gruda," the Polish word for "dirt clod."

As a student, Karol Wojtyla wrote his doctoral thesis on the Spanish mystic St. John of the Cross. Now, trying to live and teach the Gospel under communist repression, the young priest experienced St. John's dark night of the soul in a frighteningly real way. The kind of layered meditative thinking that Wojtyla discovered in St. John's writings inspired him to write several cycles of poems.

In the short poem below from Wojtyla's sequence called *Mother*, the poet speaks in Mary's voice, inviting us into prayer in an astonishing way. Using Mary's *Magnificat* from the Gospel of Luke as a departure point, he contemplates, not the words of the *Magnificat* themselves, but what those words did for Mary when she sang them. Mary speaks to God about the discovery and transformation that took place within her while she sang the words of her *Magnificat* in response to her cousin Elizabeth's greeting (Luke 1:41-45).

Before turning to this poem, we would do well to first pray with Mary the very words Fr. Wojtyla recalls her having sung in Elizabeth's presence:

> My soul proclaims the greatness of the Lord;
> my spirit rejoices in God my Savior
> for he has looked with favor on his lowly servant.
>
> From this day all generations will call me blessed:
> the Almighty has done great things for me
> and holy is his Name.
>
> He has mercy on those who fear him
> in every generation.
>
> He has shown the strength of his arm,
> and has scattered the proud in their conceit.
>
> He has cast down the mighty from their thrones,
> and has lifted up the lowly.

He has filled the hungry with good things,
and the rich he has sent away empty.

He has come to the help of his servant Israel,
for he has remembered his promise of mercy,
the promise he made to our fathers,
to Abraham and his children forever. (Luke 1:46-55)[6]

Now let us enter deeper into the experience of this song through the words of the poet-priest who imagines Mary recalling what happened to her "when the song burst out and bell-like embraced me":

The Song Opens

I didn't know myself, that self I found in song.
I walked among people, never parting their cares
from my simple acts, my womanly thoughts
always spoken aloud.

And when the song burst out and bell-like
embraced me, I saw how the words
discover your hiding place
as light melts at the center of thought.
When the song stops, hear my thoughts better.

Many long days will pass among the people,
different people—in my blood's even pulsing
I visit You in them, giving You no other song.
When the first song returns, it will rebound,
in deepest echo against all of creation—

to find its focus again in my lips' quiet whisper,
where it lasts longest,
endures at its simplest.[7]

It is tempting to read the title of this poem simply as "the song begins," but the actual title is far more instructive and powerful. Its double meaning tells us that the very act of singing the *Magnificat* "opens" Mary up to the Holy Spirit, to the transformative power of the incarnate God within her and to the profound events of salvation history that lie before her.

The poem's first four words, "I didn't know myself," are jolting given what has already taken place in Luke's gospel. The angel Gabriel has appeared to Mary to inform her that God's living Son is within her womb, and she has responded with perfect and humble obedience: "Behold, I am the hand-maid of the Lord. May it be done to me according to your word" (Luke 1:38). But Fr. Wojtyla, having heard many confessions and walked and stumbled on his own spiritual journey, appreciates the natural human bewilderment and uncertainty that Mary must have known. He appreciates the intimate assurance she was seeking in her pilgrimage to see her older cousin.

After all, one day Mary had been going about her chores and the next she learns from an angel that she is pregnant with God's Son. How could she have known "that self I found in song" when she "walked among people, never part-ing their cares / from my simple acts, my womanly thoughts / always spoken aloud"?

But then in the warm embrace of Elizabeth and in the words of the song that "burst out" and "embraced" her, Mary sees "how the words / discover your hiding place / as light melts at the center of thought." She professes in song what she has come to know, that God "has looked with favor on his lowly servant" and filled not just her hunger but the hunger of all his people "with good things" and "has remembered his promise of mercy."

Anyone who has ever professed their faith in song can appreciate the profound and comforting weight of the silence that follows when the music stops. In that silence we can pray as the poet imagines Mary to have done here: "When the song stops, hear my thoughts better."

We need only consider the extraordinary events and unspeakable suffering that lay ahead of this young mother in order to appreciate what living the words of this canticle would mean. So too with the young poet-priest from Kraków who would one day stand up as pope and confront communist oppression, and who would experience Mary's intervening grace protecting him when he was shot by an assassin in St. Peter's Square. And so too with our seemingly ordinary lives. "Many long days will pass among . . . different people—in [our] blood's even pulsing."

As those days pass, may we resolve—in the words spoken by Mary—to visit God in those people, to offer God, even in our deepest discouragement, "no other song" than "the first song" of faith we sang. May our own canticle "rebound / in deepest echo against all of creation— / to find its focus again in [our] lips' quiet whisper, / where it lasts longest, endures at its simplest." Imagine.

Part III

Gift to This Gift

A Christmas Carol

Christina Rossetti (1830–1894)

Two literary works from England's Victorian age share this illustrious title. The first, of course, is Charles Dickens's famous sentimental, moral tale of the transformed Ebenezer Scrooge that likely has much to do with the transformation of this holy religious feast into a time of making merry—or else! The other is the poem by Christina Rossetti which, having been set to music by multiple composers through the decades, has become better known by its stark opening line: "In the bleak mid-winter . . ."

For those of us who share Mr. Scrooge's repentant desire to "honor Christmas in [our] hearts," but who feel emotionally fatigued and at odds with the compulsory demands to create uninterrupted holly-jolliness for several weeks, Ms. Rossetti's four words are joltingly and refreshingly honest. From this bleakness, the famous English poetess goes on to compose a lyrical meditation on the first Christmas that places us at the wintry nativity scene she imagines, and then ends by solving the greatest gift-giving problem on our shopping list.

First published in *Scribner's Monthly* in January of 1872, Rossetti's "Carol" has been prayed in song by people for well over a century and continues to be set to music by twenty-first-century composers. The poem's most recognizable musical settings were done in the early twentieth century—one by composer Gustav Holst (by far my favorite) and another slightly less somber composition by Harold Darke.

That people around the world would still be singing her words nearly a century and a half after she penned them would have been unfathomable to Christina Rossetti, though she was acclaimed as an accomplished author in her day. The youngest daughter of a politically exiled Italian poet, Christina grew up with three talented siblings in an intellectually lively family at the height of the Victorian age near the newly opened Regent's Park in London. She was narrating stories to her family before she could write. By the age of twelve she was reading and imitating her favorite poets like John Keats, and by her late teens she was successfully shaping poems into sonnets and other verse forms. Since her brother Dante Gabriel Rossetti was a famous Pre-Raphaelite painter who used his youngest sister as a model for the Virgin Mary, Christina's religious piety is something we can behold with particular literalness today in paintings like *Ecce Ancilla Domini* (*The Annunciation*).

As a talented woman poet, Christina was seen by many in England as the successor to Elizabeth Barrett Browning, and her most famous poem "Goblin Market" has secured her place in the English canon. Nonetheless, her affiliation with the Pre-Raphaelites, her deep religious devotion within the Anglo-Catholic movement, and the Victorian sentimentality of her children's verse did little to sustain her literary reputation during the onset of the modernist movement in the early twentieth century. Freudian treatments, and more recently feminist criticism, have brought attention to her work but have also in some way obscured the fact that as a master of poetic form and expression, Christina Rossetti stands among England's greatest poets.

Her literary success was counterpoised by a life of family financial hardships, personal spiritual struggles, and broken relationships with three suitors. She experienced bouts of debilitating depression from an early age and painful illnesses as she grew older. In both the London landscape surrounding her and that of her own interior life, Christina knew all too well the place where she set her "Carol"—the "bleak mid-winter" where "frosty wind made moan" and "earth stood hard as iron / water like a stone." The "snow on snow" she imagines to have blanketed early Palestine belongs less to "long ago" and more to the layered emotions of her own life as she looked out her windows upon nineteenth-century London.

If you desire to keep Christmas in your heart and to pray words that help you know what that means, then turn with Christina Rossetti to the wintry first nativity she imagines. If you find that enlisting the music of Holst or Darke or other composers helps, then by all means cue up your favorite recording and pray on:

A Christmas Carol

In the bleak mid-winter
    Frosty wind made moan,
Earth stood hard as iron
    Water like a stone;
Snow had fallen, snow on snow,
    Snow on snow,
In the bleak mid-winter
    Long ago.

Our God, Heaven cannot hold him,
    Nor earth sustain;

Heaven and earth shall flee away
  When he comes to reign:
In the bleak mid-winter
  A stable-place sufficed
The Lord God Almighty
  Jesus Christ.

Enough for Him, whom cherubim
  Worship night and day,
A breast full of milk
  And a manger full of hay;
Enough for Him, whom angels
  Fall down before,
The ox and ass and camel
  Which adore.

Angels and archangels
  May have gathered there,
Cherubim and seraphim
  Thronged the air;
But only his mother
  In her maiden bliss
Worshiped the Beloved
  With a kiss.

What can I give Him,
  Poor as I am?
If I were a shepherd
  I would bring a lamb;
If I were a Wise Man,
  I would do my part,—
Yet what can I give Him,
  Give my heart.[1]

The softness and elegance of these stanzas all but conceal their strict form, which yields a musical quality punctuated in ten separately rhyming quatrains shaped into five thematic stanzas. What Gustav Holst in particular recognized was the prevalence of words like water, angel, and heaven that end upon a down, rather than an up-beat, and give the poem a subdued serenity. Note also the three succinct summary syllables that form the ending line of each stanza and note how each of the stanzas can be a prayer unto itself.

We are pulled into this poem by the wind and frozen water and the mesmerizing repetition of "snow on snow," an image with which we who live in northern climates are all too familiar. But where exactly is this unyielding snow and how "long ago"? The answer doesn't actually come until the fifth line of the next stanza: "A stable-place sufficed." Some have worried over the theological accuracy of Rossetti's hyperbolic claims that heaven could not hold Christ and that "Heaven and earth shall flee away / When he comes to reign." Others find a biblical referent in the book of Kings and note how the poet prophetically has readers experience the triumphant end of time even before we ponder the birth of the Christ child in Bethlehem.

In the next stanza we are brought from the hovering of cherubim back down to the frozen earth that holds a "manger full of hay" that "the ox and ass and camel . . . adore." But among these familiar images is the detail of "a breast full of milk" that conveys the profound humanness of incarnation. In his musical arrangement Harold Darke prudishly altered this line to "a heart full of mirth"—stripping the poem of a crucial maternal image that prepares us for the stirring climactic image of the next stanza.

While angels and archangels gathered with thronging cherubim to behold the newborn child, only one person in

Rossetti's verse is able to enact the most intimate act of adoration. ". . . only his mother / in her maiden bliss / Worshiped the Beloved / With a kiss." Images of Mary cradling and holding Jesus abound in art, but far fewer present this tender intimacy in which we are invited to prayerfully share.

Do we even belong in this place at such a moment? What do we do? What can we possibly offer? If we were shepherds stirred by angel song we would "bring a lamb." If we were wise men led by a star we would have packed exotic gifts. "Yet what can I give him?" is the pinnacle of this Christmas prayer. The three-word answer in the final line demands more of us than even Mr. Scrooge's pledge to keep Christmas in his heart. In this bleak mid-winter we resolve in prayer to give away our heart—with all of the joy and worry and sorrow and hope that it contains—making ourselves, in that giving, as vulnerable as the infant Child who receives us.

The Nativity of Christ

St. Robert Southwell (1561–1595)

Let's admit it. Many of us arrive at December 25 too tired to pray. Weeks of preparation and a variety of festivities can leave us physically, emotionally, and spiritually worn out for a celebration that is supposed to begin, not end, on Christmas Day. "The problem with Christmas,' my wife has often complained, "is that women have to do ninety percent of the work." And, I might add, the credit is all given to a man in a white beard. The real "war on Christmas" has little to do with whether an overworked hourly retail employee wishes me a Merry Christmas or Happy Holidays. The real skirmish is for space and time to prayerfully celebrate the incarnation of Jesus. This battle is one that was passed down to us along with that ugly sweater and has everything to do with why we find ourselves spending what should be days of spiritual preparation at retail counters and supermarkets in the first place.

So, what—when the piles of torn wrapping paper and bows are swept away, and the last scraps of ham or turkey are finally gone from the near-empty fridge, and we find ourselves empathizing with the dead tree that is beginning to drop its needles—are worn-out wassailers to do? I suggest we think like a wise man or a shepherd.

Epiphanies often come in the form of afterthoughts. Are we to believe that the shepherds and the magi who visited

Bethlehem beheld and comprehended all at once what they were beholding? Not likely. Comprehension more likely came when one shepherd asked another "What was all that commotion the other night?" Or, on the magi's journey back east, while feeding the camels or warming their feet by a fire at night. It is then that the wise men probably began to become wise. So, we still have time to behold Christmas! And William Shakespeare's very distant cousin and fellow poet, Robert Southwell, SJ, is ready to help.

Robert Southwell was a young Jesuit priest who himself lived as an outlaw in his native England. Unlike Shakespeare and others who concealed their Catholic beliefs and sympathies during an age of hazardous religious controversy, Fr. Southwell made it his life's vocation to minister to Catholics in his home country. Having been sent to the European continent as a teenager to study in Catholic schools, Robert went on to become a Jesuit priest in Rome at a time when the order itself was only four decades old. The newly ordained Southwell, was determined—despite the objections of his superiors who recognized his enormous potential as a preacher, writer, and leader—to follow in the imperiled footsteps of his fellow English Jesuits like Edmund Campion and return to his native England where a gruesome death was a near certainty. From the time he arrived clandestinely on England's shores in 1586 with his companion Fr. Henry Garnet, he spent his time maneuvering through the English Catholic underground with dexterous stealth, eluding the Queen's priest hunters, evading near capture by hiding in walls, chimneys, and cellars. Southwell and Garnet moved about in disguise at night with other priests, bringing the sacraments to imprisoned Catholics, presiding at secret Masses, and hearing confessions. They also operated an underground printing press that published homilies, catechesis, and apologetics, as well as poems by the young Robert Southwell.

Fr. Robert was eventually betrayed and captured in 1593, and after three years of torture and prolonged imprisonment he was brought to trial at his own insistence. Condemned for treason he was hanged, drawn, and quartered at Tyburn gallows in February of 1595. Within months of his death, his poetry began to proliferate from London printing presses, and during the next four decades fifteen editions of his works were printed, indicating that his popularity reached well beyond just the Catholic population. In 1970, Robert Southwell was canonized as one of the Forty Martyrs of England and Wales.

As a writer, St. Southwell was no William Shakespeare. But neither was he merely a priest trying his hand at verse. He was an excellent poet, determined, in his words, "to weave a new web in an old loom." That is, he used popular literary forms of the day to try to turn English hearts and minds away from pagan idolatry back toward the love of Christ. In retrospect we recognize that this talented young priest was a one-man English literary reformation, and against daunting odds his reformation actually succeeded in profound and lasting ways, having a notable influence not just on his cousin Shakespeare, but on many other poets as well.

Within the church and among his fellow Jesuits, Robert Southwell is most remembered for his martyrdom, but he did earn a place as a minor poet in the English canon of literature, and among his many fine works, he wrote many wonderful Christmas poems. So, as the boughs of holly, that were purchased way too soon, begin to brown, and the mayhem of the commercial frenzy subsides to relief, go find an empty room and shut the door; seek out a quiet church, or treat yourself to a walk outdoors, and let your heart give voice to these four stanzas of praise from over four centuries ago:

The Nativity of Christ

Behold the father is his daughter's son,
The bird that built the nest is hatch'd therein,
The old of years an hour hath not outrun,
Eternal life to live doth now begin,
The word is dumb, the mirth of heaven doth weep,
Might feeble is, and force doth faintly creep.

O dying souls! behold your living spring!
O dazzled eyes! behold your sun of grace!
Dull ears attend what word this word doth bring!
Up, heavy hearts, with joy your joy embrace!
From death, from dark, from deafness, from despairs,
This life, this light, this word, this joy repairs.

Gift better than Himself God doth not know,
Gift better than his God no man can see;
This gift doth here the giver given bestow,
Gift to this gift let each receiver be:
God is my gift, Himself He freely gave me,
God's gift am I, and none but God shall have me.

Man alter'd was by sin from man to beast;
Beast's food is hay, hay is all mortal flesh;
Now God is flesh, and lies in manger press'd,
As hay the brutest sinner to refresh:
Oh happy field wherein this fodder grew,
Whose taste doth us from beasts to men renew![2]

In the profound opening line of this poem, Southwell proclaims the paradox of God the Father becoming flesh by being born into the world through his daughter Mary. God was born into the very world and womb (nest) that he created. The words of the Mass, "who humbled himself to share in our humanity" are given new life in the poet's description of how the mightiest became the most vulnerable as the eternal divine began an earthly life as an infant in an improvised crib that he himself created.

In the second stanza, in response to the incomprehensible gift of the incarnation, Southwell commands his and our souls to behold our "living spring!" And our "dazzled eyes" to "behold" our "sun of grace!" and our "dull ears" to "attend" the "word this word doth bring!" He urges our "heavy hearts" to embrace "with joy [our] joy!"

In stanza three, even as the frantic month of material gift-giving leaves us exhausted and we stagger from the exchange counter with vague New Year's resolutions, Southwell encourages our joy by having us recall the only two gifts that ultimately matter: the gift that God is to us and the gift that he calls us to be for him: "God's gift am I, and none but God shall have me."

Then in the final stanza, this poet-priest draws us to the Eucharist. Cleverly reminding us that original sin transformed us into beasts and that beasts eat hay, he turns our attention to the food that now lies in that Bethlehem barn's feeding trough: the newborn Christ, the same Christ incarnated in pressed bread each Eucharist: "God is flesh, and lies in manger press'd."

Nearly 425 years ago St. Robert Southwell went to his execution proclaiming gladly the truth he expressed in this Christmas hymn. May it help lift us beyond our weariness with Christmas's political, retail, and personal battles and beckon back to the incomprehensible simplicity that is the Christmas miracle. May we find with this young poet a way "with joy [to] joy embrace!"

Ring Out, Wild Bells

Alfred Lord Tennyson (1809–1882)

"Ring out the old, ring in the new!" people routinely declare at the start of a new year, not realizing that they are quoting a line of verse from one of England's greatest poets. As to the actual action these words express, the only ringing most people are likely to hear today at the dawn of the new year will come from the unpleasant cacophonous echo between their ears on New Year's morning, or from whatever ringtone they have programmed on their phone that prompts them off the pillow into a new "calendar year" when the liturgical year is still new, the fiscal year and the academic year are both half over, and our own sense of our place in time may be understandably confounded.

For Catholics, January 1 is the feast of The Solemnity of Mary, the Holy Mother of God, a holy day of obligation in the octave of Christmas Day. We are called to worship by the ringing of church bells, the same bells that resound generously throughout the season, beckoning us to lift our eyes and ears upward from the rapid passing of our temporal days to the incarnate love and eternal truth to which we must ascend.

But when was the last time you heard or heeded the ringing of bells?

Was it the incessant chimes of the Salvation Army bell-ringer in front of the store as you rushed through the final crush of the holiday mayhem? Did those bells provoke an impatient reflex of guilt and charity that prompted you to toss in some loose change or bills and proffer a hurried Merry Christmas? Or was it the bells of your parish that provoked you? Bells alerting you to what you already knew? That you were late for Mass, bent over in the salted ice of the church parking lot trying to tie the shoe of one of your children who has also announced that he "needed to go to the potty"? "Hell's bells!" was the familiar epithet that would come from my mother's mouth at such moments. But it's a New Year! And it is heaven's, not hell's bells that ought to beckon to us—if we could only hear them.

We may recall the abundant blessings of the previous year or be impatient to be rid of its unexpected bruisings. We may tally up the gains, but also take note of the irretrievable losses. The year fades with the forgiveness we beg when we speak those familiar words each Sunday, "in what I have done and in what I have failed to do." *Mea culpa, mea culpa, mea maxima culpa!*

Most of us welcome the chance for a fresh start without any accumulated faults, what the poet Dana Gioia describes as "A calendar with every day uncrossed, / a field of snow without a single footprint"[3] With that fresh hope, and for *auld lang syne*, let's try if we can to really ring out the old and ring in the new in earnest prayer.

To help us I offer here this hymn of unrestrained New Year hope and optimism written by Alfred Lord Tennyson (1809–1892). Alfred Tennyson is counted among the greatest of Victorian poets and, to my mind, can be counted among the top five English poets ever. He spent forty-two years as England's poet laureate, was the first poet in England to ever be awarded a peerage, accepting the title "Lord" with some reluctance. He brought King Arthur and Guinevere back to life in his remarkable retelling of Arthurian legend in *Idylls of the King*, penned such classics as *Ulysses*, and is the poet who famously declared, "Better to have loved and lost / Than never to have loved at all."

Those famous lines come amid a long poem entitled *In Memoriam* in which Tennyson laments for many, many pages the loss of his dear friend and would-be brother-in-law, Arthur Hallam. In that same long poem, after 105 sections of unyielding grief and sorrow at Hallam's death, Tennyson, all of a sudden, bursts forth in the Christmas season with the psalm-like hymn below. In doing so he tries to put aside his "[private] grief that saps the mind" as well as the public "party strife," "civic slander" and the "feud of rich and poor."

The poet is exuberant in his celebration of Christ's birth and in welcoming the New Year it signals. He stands amid the great Christmas feasts and shouts out his hope for better days ahead. The stanzas culminate in the hope of Christ's triumphant return and the world's redemption. To gain the full effect of these words you must prepare to let go of the most significant private and public sorrows of this past year, populate your imagination with the pealing of the most glorious bells you have ever heard, and then join Tennyson in his fervent prayer:

Section 106 of In Memoriam

Ring out, wild bells, to the wild sky,
    The flying cloud, the frosty light:
    The year is dying in the night;
Ring out, wild bells, and let him die.

Ring out the old, ring in the new,
 Ring, happy bells, across the snow:
 The year is going, let him go;
Ring out the false, ring in the true.

Ring out the grief that saps the mind
 For those that hear we see no more;
 Ring out the feud of rich and poor,
Ring in redress to all mankind.

Ring out a slowly dying cause,
 And ancient forms of party strife;
 Ring in the nobler modes of life,
With sweeter manners, purer laws.

Ring out the want, the care, the sin,
 The faithless coldness of the times;
 Ring out, ring out my mournful rhymes
But ring the fuller minstrel in.

Ring out false pride in place and blood,
 The civic slander and the spite;
 Ring in the love of truth and right,
Ring in the common love of good.

Ring out old shapes of foul disease;
 Ring out the narrowing lust of gold;
 Ring out the thousand wars of old,
Ring in the thousand years of peace.

Ring in the valiant man and free,
 The larger heart, the kindlier hand;
 Ring out the darkness of the land,
Ring in the Christ that is to be.[4]

Those of us who can or must begin the year in mid-winter will make first footprints in yet unblemished snow; others do so in sand or on still un-trampled ground. Wherever and however we step forward into a new year we know our lives might begin afresh and that the days ahead assuredly hold surprises, small triumphs, and unforeseen disappointments. But how, as we step from the fleeting and impersonal jubilance of strangers at Time's Square and make our private way through the slowly lengthening days of warmth and light, can we hope to "ring out the thousand wars of old" and ring in "the thousand years of peace"?

How can we "ring out the want, the care, the sin"? It will take more than bells to achieve such mighty aspirations. Tennyson knew this very well, as did John Lennon when he composed "Imagine." Our longing for all things to be just and right in our own fraught and fragile lives, as well as in the whole wide world, is not mere naiveté. It is in fact the force and power contained in three words Jesus commanded us to pray: "Thy kingdom come." Wherever our footsteps take us we are called to summon up enough hope and faith to "Ring out the darkness of the land" and to "Ring in the Christ that is to be."

Bells of all kinds, even ringtones I suppose, can remind us of this. May whatever "wild bells" we hear ringing in whatever "wild sk[ies]" we walk beneath become sudden prayers of our own in which we beg the grace to sound our days with "nobler modes of life," to "the common love of good," to "the love of truth and right," and to "the larger heart, the kindlier hand."

Part IV

To Earth and Ashes

Sonnet 4, O My Black Soul

John Donne (1572–1631)

"Ask not for whom the bell tolls," warns the poet in one of the most ominous spiritual admonishments ever written, "it tolls for *thee*." The warning is part of a meditation in which John Donne instructs us that when we hear the bell tolling someone's imminent death we should not send to ask who is dying, but resolve instead that the bell is tolling for us. We may feel perfectly healthy, but death awaits us all sooner than we expect. Besides, he argues, we are all a small part of the human whole and "each man's death diminishes me." Church bells rarely ring out to mark a person's passing these days, but phones do still ring suddenly in the middle of the night and funeral processions and ambulances still occasionally pass us by. Dr. Donne would not have us turn back to our affairs smug in the fact that we are still breathing, but instead recognize how close our own death is—and make ready.

In the sonnet below, Donne dramatizes—with all of the terrifying angst engendered by the pervasive disease and political imprisonments of his age—the perilous spiritual predicament he believes we all face. It may or may not be a consolation to know that the poem ends with a clever triumph of theological wit. John Donne is nothing if not clever, and oftentimes his impressive wit can displace the expected seriousness his subject seems to demand. Religion and its contents, however, were no laughing matter for a young Catholic zealot turned eventual Anglican priest and Dean of St. Paul's in London.

Donne was born into a notoriously Roman Catholic family in England at a time when practice of that religion was effectively prohibited (see the section on Robert Southwell). His mother was the niece of St. Thomas More. Two of his uncles were Jesuit priests, and Donne and his brother Henry were sent to Oxford as young men with their Catholic identities carefully concealed. Not long afterwards, Henry died in a London prison soon after being arrested for harboring a Catholic priest in his apartment. A rash and ill-advised marriage to his young wife Anne made the promising young Donne something of a political and professional outcast, and while joining the clergy was not necessarily a last resort, it was what King James insisted was his best course. The brilliant preaching Donne did in this role would seem to confirm the King's opinion. It was after his ordination that he authored the Holy Sonnets and other religious poems that stand in contrast to the sexually cavalier poems of his youth that the eminent Dr. Donne dismissed as the work of young "Jack" Donne.

If you have ever tried to talk yourself into going to confession or even carried for weeks or months or years something that weighs heavily upon your conscience, then you can imagine an earnest conversation between you and your soul in which the diagnosis you provide evokes the pressing need and desire for repentance.

Sonnet 4, O My Black Soul

O, my black soul, now thou art summoned
By sickness, Death's herald and champion;
Thou'rt like a pilgrim, which abroad hath done
Treason, and durst not turn to whence he's fled;

Or like a thief, which till death's doom be read,
Wisheth himself deliver'd from prison,
But damn'd and haled to execution,
Wisheth that still he might be imprisoned.
Yet grace, if thou repent, thou canst not lack;
But who shall give thee that grace to begin?
O, make thyself with holy mourning black,
And red with blushing, as thou art with sin;
Or wash thee in Christ's blood, which hath this
    might,
That being red, it dyes red souls to white.[1]

That this poem is written in a the form of an Italian son-net with subtle feminine rhymes comprising the octave (first eight lines) and stark monosyllabic rhymes in its sestet (final six lines) makes the poem's two parts abundantly clear: "O, my black soul" you are in serious peril; "Yet grace, if thou repent" may save you.

"Summoned by sickness," the speaker's soul has no good options. He is like a pilgrim who has committed treason and can't return home without facing death, or like an imprisoned thief who called to the gallows now wishes he could stay in prison. He can be saved only by grace and repentance. Easily said, not easily accomplished. For always when we need to change, to repent, to end a habit, seek help for an addiction, beg forgiveness of someone, or even harder, forgive someone who has harmed us; always when we need to get right with God, when we need to seek "Amazing Grace," we first need "that grace to begin." And where to find that?

Fear is a strong motivator certainly, and though that is where this poem begins, in the clever progression of colors that leads to its conclusion, it is not fear of death or damna-tion that drives the soul to repent, but the encouragement and assurance of forgiveness. If the soul is truly remorseful—black with mourning and red with blushing—grace will come. The poem's punchline renders the paradox that the red blood of Christ turns red sin-stained souls to clean white ones. Donne's cleverness may or may not motivate our souls, but the sonnet can surely inspire the private conversation we may need to have with our own pilgrim souls.

Hogs and Salvation

Fr. Kilian McDonnell, OSB (b. 1921)

We are all familiar with the parable of the Prodigal Son. As with many biblical stories, most of us are so familiar with the story that we may not hear it anymore. Or see it. Or taste or touch it. And we have likely never considered its smell. Enter one of my favorite living poets. Fr. Kilian McDonnell, OSB, a monk of Saint John's Abbey in Minnesota for nearly seven decades, is someone you will be glad you met. An accomplished theologian, Fr. Kilian spent decades teaching at Saint John's University, publishing scholarly theological articles and books, and of course preaching thousands of homilies and ministering pastorally and sacramentally to thousands of people. Then over a quarter century ago, at the young age of seventy-five, he began writing poems.

"Could a seventy-five-year-old man shift to the less logical, more metaphorical, evocative mode and become a competent poet?" Fr. Kilian asked himself. Three stirring and inspiring books of poetry later, that question can be answered with a resolute "yes" that offers all of us hope for what we might achieve in our latter years. This monk, priest, scholar, and poet has fashioned poems that contain his vast biblical and theological knowledge in their bones and sinews; poems that sound the notes of his mischievous Irish wit and Midwestern earthiness in their voice, and poems that yield the fruits of his long contemplative life in their depiction of the personal human struggle to know God. "I wrestle with God 'flesh to flesh, sweat to mystery,' and I limp away," he says.[2] And as he does so, he leaves us provocative treasures like the one here.

In the poem "Hogs and Salvation," from his volume *Yahweh's Other Shoe*, we hear from the prodigal son, who now "strangely sober" stands knee-deep in the stench and filth of the pig sty, with an empty stomach and a broken spirit—contemplating his options:

Hogs and Salvation

So [the younger son] went and hired himself out to one of the citizens of that country, who sent him to his fields to feed the pigs. Luke 15:15

I'm strangely sober, my last shekel
gone on tavern girls and booze.
A Gentile in golden tasseled mantle
was looking for a boy to tend his piggery.

Why not? Hunger is lean.
Ask no Torah questions
when the sty is your address.

When the short-legged devils roll
in foulest mud, you forget they're smart.
Sows drop fecal cookies on my feet,
hell's latrine. Stench clings like identity.

No wonder the seven Maccabean
brothers chose death to swallowing
Greek pork. Wise men.

No boss-man lives beside this outhouse;
my castle of despair is downwind.

Will I starve in swill to my knees while
meat in my father's cupboard goes uneaten?

Why does an empty stomach
teach what Father's dumbest slave
knows after one day in his house?

The wide door stands always open,
the pantry shelves are never empty,
unprocurable wine from Spain in barrels.
The old man's been expecting company.[3]

Jesus tells the parable of the prodigal to instruct his listeners about the folly of our journey into sin and the great readiness of God the Father to forgive us and rejoice at our return to his abundant love. Fr. Kilian invites us to listen in on the thoughts of this younger son, who having spent the last of his money "on tavern girls and booze" stands in the "foulest mud" of "hell's latrine," slowly coming to his emotional, rational, and moral senses. Kilian the theologian would have us consider along the way something that we probably hadn't thought of before. Namely, that since Hebrew law prohibited the consumption of pork, tending pigs would not only be physically filthy work, but an assault upon this young Jewish man's religious and cultural sensibilities. Yet, it is the very kind of desperate necessity that sin brings one to: "Ask no Torah questions / when the sty is your address."

If the predicament and pleas of this prodigal were his plight alone this poem would be just a colorful glimpse into a familiar story and certainly no prayer of ours. But in a season of our lives that calls us to contrition, be that season liturgical or personal, we should try, like the wayward young man in this poem, to be honest with ourselves about our situation. Most of us, at one time or another, have felt entitled to more than what we have. We have looked at the poor hand we have been dealt and declared to ourselves that we deserve more. Many of us have followed our pride and ambition toward tantalizing options or glittering opportunities only to find ourselves far from our Father, filled with disappointment, anger, and resentment. Who among us has not found themselves standing in life's muck with "fecal cookies" dropping at our feet? And most of us know what it is like to be downwind of life's stink, holed up in a "castle of despair" of our own making.

The poet, who has been shaped in part by listening as a confessor to the voices and hearts of hundreds of penitents, invites us with his poem to contemplate our own spiritual hunger and to recall what even our "Father's dumbest slave / knows after one day in his house." Namely, that God's grace is as abundant and lavish as "unprocurable wine from Spain in barrels" and his "wide door stands always open."

Several years ago I met Fr. Kilian for the first time. I found myself walking on a winter morning on the campus of Saint John's campus after having just purchased his two most recent books at the bookstore. My wife and I came upon an old monk bundled in a coat and scarf, shuffling down the sidewalk out of a winter mist. Who else? The poet himself. It was a providential meeting, marked by hospitality, warmth, and laughter. In retrospect, I could say it felt like the last line of this poem: "The old man's been expecting company." Last year I paid him an unexpected visit. We had a nice chat in his room until he grew tired. When I left he said, "Tell people I'm still writing, but not to hold their breath."

We needn't hold our breath in anticipation or worry. Fr. Kilian has given us what we need to pray our way back to our Father's house. Whatever muck you find yourselves standing in these days; whatever resentful thoughts you have swirling in your mind because of the world's inevitable disappointments; whatever "stench" you feel clinging to your identity, let this poem remind you in a vivid and poignant way that you need not starve in swill to your knees when God's pantry shelves are full and his "wide door stands always open." It is always a good time to swallow your pride, find fresh air to breathe, and head to the open doors of your home. After all, you are the very company the old man is expecting.

The Litany

Dana Gioia (b. 1950)

Of all the church's seasons, it seems to me that Lent is always the most personal. We may progress liturgically through forty days together, it is true, but we also walk alone. Starting with the intimate thumb smudge of ashes on our very own forehead, the journey is an inward and a private one. Our own failings, our own losses, our own loneliness. This is what we measure and lament. Our sacrifices are ones we are urged to make in private, and the Scripture stories we read all show us how reconciliation, from Galilee to Gethsemane, takes place on the most personal terms.

And of course, penitential seasons can arrive in our lives at any time, unexpected, long-postponed, and can last for well over forty days. As we struggle toward personal redemption during slowly lengthening days of spring, or over months and years of struggle, it is imperative that we recognize that, isolated as we may feel, we are not struggling alone. Penitential purple is a communal fashion. Our losses and longings are shared with the people we love as well as the people we struggle to love. The poem below is "a litany to earth and ashes, / to the dust of roads and vacant rooms" by the contemporary, award-winning poet and critic, Dana Gioia.

A litany, of course, is a form of responsive petition used in liturgy. From the Greek words *litē* (supplication) and *litanela* (prayer), litanies can be as much a part of private devotions as public prayer. At first, Gioia's "The Litany" may seem anything but a prayer to encourage us on our journey, but as with any prayer one must hear it and speak it with the heart. And in this case several times.

I have been fortunate over the past decade to spend some time in conversation and correspondence with Mr. Gioia and have come to appreciate him not just as an exceptional poet, but as one of the more profound artistic voices of our age. A writer who has achieved international recognition for his work, Dana Gioia is also a Catholic who has endured profound personal loss. He speaks honestly of the experiences he has known and genuinely as the person those experiences have made him. "Catholics don't minimize the struggle and the difficulty of life's journey," Gioia insists. "They have a sense of a moral and spiritual journey; they have a sense of human imperfection—original sin is an essential tenant of the Catholic world view." As a poet and a Catholic, Gioia understands and exhibits in his work the reality that transcendence toward the eternal happens through our everyday material world. "Catholics," he says, "see a relationship between the material and the non-material world. They have a Sacramental sense, and Catholic writers have a sense of their own sinfulness, their own inability to measure up to their goals without the avenue of grace."[4]

With these thoughts of the poet as preparation, you can now come personally to this litany. You might wish to save it for a moment on your penitential journey when the road seems especially alone, long, and hard.

The Litany

This is a litany of lost things,
a canon of possessions dispossessed,
a photograph, an old address, a key.

It is a list of words to memorize
or to forget—of *amo*, *amas*, *amat*,
the conjugations of a dead tongue
in which the final sentence has been spoken.

This is the liturgy of rain,
falling on mountain, field, and ocean—
indifferent, anonymous, complete—
of water infinitesimally slow,
sifting through rock, pooling in darkness,
gathering in springs, then rising without our agency,
only to dissolve in mist or cloud or dew.

This is a prayer to unbelief,
to candles guttering and darkness undivided,
to incense drifting into emptiness.
It is the smile of a stone Madonna
and the silent fury of the consecrated wine,
a benediction on the death of a young god,
brave and beautiful, rotting on a tree.

This is a litany to earth and ashes,
to the dust of roads and vacant rooms,
to the fine silt circling in a shaft of sun,
settling indifferently on books and beds.
This is a prayer to praise what we become,
"Dust thou art, to dust thou shalt return."
Savor its taste—the bitterness of earth and ashes.

This is a prayer, inchoate and unfinished,
for you, my love, my loss, my lesion,
a rosary of words to count out time's
illusions, all the minutes, hours, days
the calendar compounds as if the past
existed somewhere—like an inheritance
still waiting to be claimed.

Until at last it is our litany, *mon vieux,*
my reader, my voyeur, as if the mist
streaming from the gorge, this pure paradox,
the shattered river rising as it falls—
splintering the light, swirling it skyward,
neither transparent nor opaque but luminous,
even as it vanishes—were not our life.[5]

Before you read "The Litany" a second time, note how the poet uses the resonant repetitive chant of a litany to catalogue and consider the everyday losses we all experience: "a photograph, an old address, a key." Note how he ponders the ephemeral wonders of nature all around us, like "the liturgy of rain, / falling on mountain, field, and ocean." Hear how truthfully he acknowledges the hollow discouragement we feel when our faith is dry and we stand or kneel amid "candles guttering and darkness undivided" and "incense drifting into emptiness." Our unbelief too, he knows, belongs to God and is worthy of prayer.

"This is a prayer to praise what we become," declares the poet before reciting the familiar Ash Wednesday refrain: "Dust thou art, to dust thou shalt return." He would have us remember not only our inevitable mortality, but to make that mortality our prayer, to "Savor its taste—the bitterness of earth and ashes." That bitterness, however, is but the prelude to redemption, to the grace that is our "inheritance / still waiting to be claimed." And ultimately, Gioia turns to us his readers, calling us *"mon vieux"* ("old chap"), reminding us that we are not walking this spiritual journey alone. The driest dust on the road of our journey is shared by all humanity, and especially those who struggle most. But so too is the "pure paradox" of our physical and spiritual existence like "the shattered river rising as it falls— / splintering the light, swirling it skyward, / neither transparent nor opaque but luminous, / even as it vanishes . . ."

The private litanies and refrains of our own lives are peculiar to ourselves. Gioia would have us see the world around us in sacramental terms: the minutes, hours, and days; the everyday losses, as well as the incomplete sentences and unfinished prayers. Ultimately even our unfinished prayers and daily worries bring us back to "the silent fury of the consecrated wine, / a benediction on the death of a young god, / brave and beautiful, rotting on a tree." The redemption wrought by Christ's suffering and death on the cross is at once universally shared by all and, like the individual failings marked by ashes on our own forehead, deeply personal. "At last it is *our* litany."

All Creation Wept

Melissa Range (b. 1973)

It is always wise before embarking on a journey to consider where it is we hope to arrive. Inevitable delays and detours are more bearable if we at least have a destination in sight. In the case of our spiritual journeys like the one many of us try to make through forty days of Lent, we may say that we are moving toward a more whole and reconciled self or we may want something more orthodox and specific like progress toward the paschal mystery of Christ's suffering, death, and resurrection. Such destinations, however, may seem abstract and unattainable from the edge of winter where the arrival of spring itself still seems improbable. We may set off on our journey ready to welcome the detours.

One good prayer may be all we need to help us understand where we are going and to help keep us on the path. So how about if we forego the more abstract destinations above and resolve that the Lenten journey takes us to the cross.

Our guide on this journey is Melissa Range, a contemporary poet who teaches at Lawrence University in Wisconsin. Raised in the Appalachian region of East Tennessee, Melissa was surrounded by and steeped in nature as well as Bible stories from an early age. She has spent her life discovering the powerful intersection of lived experience with the spoken and written word. She earned an MFA in writing, forming as she did a special affinity for the poetry of Gerard Manley Hopkins. She studied in divinity school, worked with refugee children as an Americorps volunteer, and ultimately earned a PhD in literature from the University of Missouri.

Along the way Melissa published two collections of poetry. *Horse and Rider*, which won the 2010 Walt McDonald Prize, and *Scriptorium*. Some of her poetry is more explicitly religious than others; all of it depicts the wounds of violence and the paradoxical tension between worldly power and human frailty. One of my favorites is "The Conversion of Saul Imagined as a Scene in a Western." The law-enforcing Saul, wearing a "white ten-gallon" hat, is "shot from the saddle" in the "high noon light" by a stranger he cannot see. The stranger's voice sinks "into Saul like blood into the dust" when he tells his persecutor: "Best hand in your badge . . . Ain't room for the two of us in any town." Saul awakes "without a scratch, a black hat by his head—an outlaw, an apostle, a changed and wanted man."[6]

"I definitely think poems can be used as devotional tools," Melissa has assured me, and I know that my own appreciation of St. Paul's encounter on the road to Damascus and his radical turn from enforcing the law of the land to becoming an outlaw for Christ has been permanently changed and reinvigorated by this poem. Let's see if she can do the same for the seminal event of the gospels that we have "heard" so many times that we may no longer *see* its significance.

One of the earliest Christian poems in the English language is the lengthy seventh-century dream vision, *Dream of the Rood*, in which the poet (likely the Benedictine Caedmon), describes a dream where the wooden cross of Christ appears to him and speaks of the suffering that it empathetically endured during the crucifixion of Jesus. With her eyes on this ancient poem and the devotional tradition from which it sprang, Professor Range offers the powerful meditation below. In doing so, she steers us toward the events of Good Friday with a renewed alertness:

All Creation Wept

And not just those disciples
whom he loved, and not just
his mother; for all creation

was his mother, if he shared
his cells with worms and ferns
and whales, silt and spiderweb,

with the very walls of his crypt.
Of all creation, only he slept,
the rest awake and rapt with grief

when love's captain leapt
onto the cross, into an abyss
the weather hadn't dreamt.

Hero mine the beloved,
cried the snowflakes, cried the moons
of unknown planets, cried the thorns

in his garland, the nails bashed
through his bones, the spikes of dry grass
on the hillside, dotted with water

and with blood—real tears,
and not a trick of rain-light
blinked and blurred onto a tree

so that the tree seems wound
in gold. It was not wound
in gold or rain but in a rapture

of salt, the wood splintering
as he splintered when he wept
over Lazarus, over Jerusalem,

until his sorrow became his action,
his grief his victory—
until his tears became a rupture

in nature, all creation
discipled to his suffering
on the gilded gallows-tree,

the wood which broke beneath the weight
of love, though it had no ears to hear
him cry out, and no eyes to see.[7]

Remarkably, what the poet achieves here is the very thing that St. Francis did in his canticle to creation and his innovation of the manger crèches that we display in our homes and churches at Christmas. She reminds us that just as "all creation" (oxen, donkeys, sheep, stars) partook in Christ's birth, so too "all creation" witnessed and was moved by his violent death. And "all creation" is not a mere abstraction since Christ "shared / his cells with worms and ferns / and whales, silt and spiderweb."

Range would have us consider that "when love's captain leapt / onto the cross" it was "the snowflakes"; "the moons / of unknown planets" far away and "the thorns" piercing his very head that cried out: "*Hero mine the beloved.*" She would have us feel "the nails bashed / through his bones" and see "the spikes of dry grass / on the hillside, dotted with water / and with blood." She would have us know that those tears were "real tears / of salt" just like ours. She would have us hear "the wood splintering" just as Jesus "splintered when

he wept / over Lazarus, over Jerusalem." Like Hopkins be-
fore her, Range converts a too-familiar noun into a verb so
that we might hear it again for the first time. "All creation"
she tells us, was "*discipled* to his suffering / on the gilded
gallows-tree."

Our journeys may be private and personal, but Melissa
Range reminds us that, like Christ, we share our destinies,
our griefs, our victories, our joy, and our discipleship with
"all creation." This is a poem to carry with us on our way. It
takes up little room in our luggage and it contains so many
ready prayers to make our own and keep us headed toward
our destination. Let us pray to be "discipled to his suffering."
Let us pray for our salt tears to be joined with Christ's and
"all creation." And let us pray simply and frequently: "*Hero
mine the beloved.*"

Part V
To Carry Him With Us

Emmaus: Christ Between

Rev. Rowan Williams (b. 1950)

Beginning with the grief-stricken Mary Magdalene's conversation with "a gardener" at the empty tomb, encounters with the risen Christ offer some of the most stirring and intriguing narratives in the gospels. Each one presents a casual collision between the physical and the metaphysical, between what we know to be true and what we cannot comprehend, between the eternal God and the bewildered ones he loves. And like the stunned resolution of Thomas after putting his fingers into the wounds of his risen teacher, each encounter culminates in a paradoxical mix of terror and joy, the simple and profound recognition: "My Lord and my God!"

Take the case of two grieving and discouraged disciples of Jesus walking together on a road for seven miles to the village of Emmaus. They are joined on their journey by a stranger with whom they share the news of their dire predicament and heartfelt grief. After hearing them speak, the stranger effectively schools them in the Hebrew scriptures, reminding them that all that has happened back in Jerusalem was necessary and good. Only after they have extended the stranger the hospitality of joining them for the night, only at table where bread and wine are shared, only then do they recognize their companion as Christ and begin to understand

76

why their hearts were burning within them as they walked down the road hearing him speak.

A beautiful reimagining of this powerful gospel story from Luke 24 is rendered by a poet who wears the auspicious title of Baron Williams of Oystermouth. This eminent moniker conveys the prestige and public achievements of the scholarly churchman it describes, but at the same time it belies this Welshman's spiritual grounded-ness. The keen intellect that has made him an accomplished academician and teacher is balanced by his devotion to God, by his love of language (he speaks three languages fluently and has good facility with at least nine others), his love of the poets from his native Wales, and his skill as a poet himself. Rev. Williams is best known to people worldwide for his decade of service as the head of the Anglican Church in his role as archbishop of Canterbury. People may remember him at the center of controversy as he struggled to prevent the Anglican Church from schism, or recall him at happier moments as when he presided at the wedding of Prince William and his bride Kate Middleton. Rowan spent much of his life studying, teaching, and administering at Cambridge and Oxford universities and today is the chancellor of the University of South Wales.

In addition to dozens of books of scholarly commentary, spiritual guidance, and translations, Rev. Williams has published several books of poetry. *The Poems of Rowan Williams* (2004) was longlisted for the Wales Book of the Year. A 2006 tribute anthology entitled *I Have Called You Friends: Reflections on Reconciliation in Honor of Frank T. Griswold* contains Williams's poetic retelling of the Emmaus event below, where the poet depicts "Christ Between" two traveling companions. Luke's gospel identifies one of the travelers on that journey as Cleopas. His unnamed companion, contemporary biblical scholars have suggested, may have been a woman, or even his wife. Such intimacy, joined by greater intimacy, is something we may imagine as we listen to Cleopas try to describe what occurred:

Emmaus: Christ Between

First the sun, then the shadow,
so that I screw my eyes to see
my friend's face, and its lines seem
different, and the voice shakes in the hot air.
Out of the rising white dust, feet
tread a shape, and, out of step,
another flat sound, stamped between voice
and ears, dancing in the gaps, and dodging
where words and feet do not fall.

When our eyes meet, I see bewilderment
(like mine); we cannot learn
this rhythm we are asked to walk,
and what we hear is not each other.
Between us is filled up, the silence
is filled up, lines of our hands
and faces pushed into shape
by the solid stranger, and the static
breaks up our waves like dropped stones.

So it is necessary to carry him with us,
cupped between hands and profiles,
so that the table is filled up, and as
the food is set and the first wine splashes,
a solid thumb and finger tear the thunderous
grey bread. Now it is cold, even indoors;
and the light falls sharply on our bones;
the rain breathes out hard, dust blackens,
and our released voices shine with water.[1]

"What was it like?" the other disciples must have demanded more than once of Cleopas and his companion once they returned to Jerusalem. What can you say of something that makes no sense whatever, and yet makes pure and perfect sense out of all the confusion you have ever known? The explanation is inadequate to those seeking material details: "another flat sound, stamped between voice / and ears, dancing in the gaps, and dodging / where words and feet do not fall." The two companions are at once walking and conversing with the risen Lord and simultaneously unaware of what is going on and who this stranger is that has joined them on the road. The poet gives voice to their perplexity in words that resound with all of us who try to walk with Christ: "we cannot learn / this rhythm we are asked to walk."

As they stumble forward out of step with the stranger, "the silence" between them "is filled up" and the realness of the experience and the impact it is having upon them is felt by the "lines of our hands / and faces pushed into shape / by the solid stranger." In Luke's account the two companions urge the stranger to stay with them when they reach Emmaus "because the day is now far spent," but Rowan illuminates the motives within their invitation: "So it is necessary to carry him with us, / cupped between hands and profiles, / so that the table is filled up . . ." They dared not let this encounter end. It was too powerful, too special. And when at table "the first wine splashes" and "a solid thumb and finger tear the thunderous / grey bread" the room turns cold and "the light falls sharply on our bones." Rain begins to fall hard, blackening the dust and the two stunned travelers "released voices shine with water." Whatever utterance their voices formed in that moment of stunned recognition, we can imagine it to be some version of "My Lord and my God!"

Oh for such an encounter as that! We pray for it, we long for it, as we spend our lives clumsily trying to learn "this rhythm we are asked to walk." Our clearest visions, like that of Cleopas and his companion, seem always to be retrospective; after the fact, once we have had time to consider things. Only then do we understand and appreciate the light that seemed to fall "sharply on our bones." How many roads have we walked down in our life without comprehending who we were with or what was truly being said until that encounter had vanished from our lives?

As we pray the words of the great old spiritual "Just a Closer Walk with Thee" may that prayer—as we walk despondently toward Emmaus or ecstatically back to Jerusalem, and on all the roads between—be filled with the truth Cleopas and his companion came to know from the stranger walking between them: "it is necessary to carry him with us."

St. Peter and the Angel

Denise Levertov (1923–1997)

We desire the Easter season to be a time of rolling back the great tombstones of our hearts, shaking off the shroud of a long penitential season and preparing to ignite our spirits in the fires of Pentecost. If we achieve this with only limited success, we may take heart in the imperfections of those who came before us.

Liturgically, this is the season when readings from the Hebrew scriptures are replaced by passages from the Acts of the Apostles. There we hear accounts of the challenges, conflicts, adventures, and bold actions of our earliest Christian ancestors. We hear again of the conversion and subsequent preaching of St. Paul, as well as the steadfast leadership and preaching of St. Peter. We learn of the conflict over circumcision and baptism, and the shortcomings of people in places like Ephesus. Both apostles struggled to spread the Good News, and both would eventually meet with violent ends doing so. The bold actions of Peter and Paul have captured the imaginations of poets and artists through the ages.

The poem below was written by a twentieth-century poet and activist who struggled in her own life's journey before becoming a Catholic just a few years before her death. It is the only poem I know that renders a poetic depiction of Peter's escape from prison as recorded in Acts 12.

To consider this poem and the thought and prayer it can inspire in us, it helps to know a little bit about the life journey of the poet, Denise Levertov (1923–1997). It is no exaggeration to say that this woman was born a poet, political activist, and a religious seeker. All three of these dispositions and destinies were in Denise from an early age and remained in her until her courageous death. Her father, a Russian Hassidic Jew and professor at Leipzig University, was placed in house arrest during World War I as an "enemy alien." After the war he immigrated to England, converted, and became an Anglican minister. Denise's mother came from Wales and together the family engaged in progressive political causes, so that young Denise not only witnessed her father's eloquence at the church pulpit, but saw her parents and sister speaking from soapboxes in the street against various forms of political oppression. Schooled at home, she was introduced to writing, music, dance, and languages, and at five years old Denise made the precocious declaration that she was going to be a writer. To the world's great benefit, she made good on her declaration.

In the late 1940s Levertov married and came to the United States, where she would spend the rest of her life dividing her time between the country's two coasts as a writer, teacher, and political activist. Ms. Levertov's spiritual journey, inspired from an early age by her father's scholarly and personal devotions and her subsequent exposure to varieties of mysticism, informed her art throughout her life and particularly after she formally converted to Christianity in 1984. At about this time she came to the conclusion that poetry and beauty and politics were incompatible, and her work began to shift much more decidedly toward religious themes. In the early 1990s Denise was received into the Roman Catholic Church in Seattle. Still actively engaged as a writer and speaker, she died in 1997 from complications from lymphoma at the age of seventy-four.

In "St. Peter and the Angel" published in *Oblique Prayers* the same year as her conversion to Christianity, we behold how Levertov' s lifelong journey of conversion, and the accompanying surprise, bewilderment, and challenges of encountering God's presence informed her art. Acts 12 tells us that upon being told by the angel to put on his belt and sandals and cloak, Peter "followed him out, not realizing that what was happening through the angel was real; he thought he was seeing a vision" (Acts 12:9). Imagine now with Levertov just what Peter must have experienced in this event:

St. Peter and the Angel

Delivered out of raw continual pain,
smell of darkness, groans of those others
to whom he was chained—

unchained, and led
past the sleepers,
door after door silently opening—
out!
And along a long street's
majestic emptiness under the moon:

one hand on the angel's shoulder, one
feeling the air before him,
eyes open but fixed . . .

And not till he saw the angel had left him,
alone and free to resume
the ecstatic, dangerous, wearisome roads of
what he had still to do,

not till then did he recognize
this was no dream. More frightening
than arrest, than being chained to his warders:
he could hear his own footsteps suddenly.
Had the angel's feet
made any sound? He could not recall.
No one had missed him, no one was in pursuit.
He himself must be
the key, now, to the next door,
the next terrors of freedom and joy.[2]

What Levertov does in this depiction of Peter's dramatic rescue is to place immediately before our senses the literal elements of captivity: the "smell of darkness" (darkness has an odor?!) and the "groans of those others" in chains. And while most of us have never been chained before, the pain the poem describes is not entirely unfamiliar to many readers. Anyone who has experienced a prolonged illness, grief, or other kind of suffering feels the poem's opening line, "delivered out of raw continual pain." We all long for the feeling of sudden liberation, if only from our everyday worries. We yearn for the hopeful experience of "door after door silently opening—out!"

But what comes after our liberation? After the angel's departure Peter realizes that he is "alone and free to resume / the ecstatic, dangerous, wearisome roads of / what he still had to do"—namely pursue the same public evangelization on behalf of the risen Jesus that got him tossed in jail in the first place. Suddenly, his own footsteps after the silent and mystic delivery by the angel, are "more frightening / than arrest, than being chained to his warders." Why does Levertov imagine the rock of our church as so suddenly frightened after his miraculous escape?

For one thing, she knows this saint well from Scriptures where time and again we see Peter swing from moments of ecstatic revelation like walking on water to the sinking reality of his frail humanity. Here as he considers what lay before him, Peter realizes that he was not liberated for his own benefit, but for the benefit of others: "He himself must be / the key, now, to the next door, / the next terrors of freedom and joy." Consider his subsequent sufferings and death from which no angel would free him.

What had been Peter's prayer as he lay on the prison floor? Aren't most of us inclined to pray for doors to be opened for us, rather than praying that we ourselves may be a key to open doors for others? Contemplating what God asks of us as we step from our various dungeons, might we not be frightened by the sound of our own footsteps? Levertov invites us to share in Peter's experience and in her own: to pray for the courage to face, for the sake of others, "the next terrors of freedom and joy."

Love III

George Herbert (1593–1633)

Several years ago, when the words and phrases of the Catholic liturgy were revised to restore some of the language closer to its original meaning, most of us struggled to get the new words right. Today, most of us don't give it a second thought. New and different? Old and restored? No matter, the words of the Mass have once more become as familiar as slipping on a pair of Sunday shoes, which may be a good thing—or not.

After all, ritual is just the more thoughtful and profound cousin of routine. And as creatures of our cherished habits, we need to be disrupted in order to stay awake and attentive to life's wonders, to the needs all around us, and to the quiet and beckoning voice of God. It's one of the things poetry does.

One of the changes in the words of the liturgy that perplexed many people (an eight out of ten on the eye-roll scale as I recall) was one that I welcomed and still cherish. Before receiving Communion Catholics used to say "Lord, I am not worthy to receive you, but only say the word and I shall be healed." That was fine for all those decades, but then this prayer was restored to the close paraphrase of Mathew 8:8, where, in an act of unbridled faith, a Roman centurion (an officer who, as he notes, commands others), approaches Jesus and asks him to heal his servant. Without any hesitation, Jesus replies, "I will go and cure him." But the centurion replies with words now familiar to us: "Lord, I am not worthy to have you enter under my roof; only say the word and my servant will be healed."

In order to profess our unworthiness to receive Jesus in the Eucharist, we repeat (already mechanically!) these words of the centurion. What these new-old words emphasize so beautifully is what is actually happening in Communion: our messy, uncleaned houses notwithstanding, Christ is coming in! He is entering under the roof of our bodies—and he is coming in to heal!

It should give any household pause.

To help us reflect on the significance of this sacramental event, I offer here the words of George Herbert. Four centuries ago Rev. Herbert, an Anglican priest and poet of remarkable talents, forsook a life of public prominence in order to live and work as a simple country pastor. His piety and humility among his parishioners—which concealed his enormous intellect as well as great internal spiritual struggles—earned him the nickname "Holy Mr. Herbert." He died at a young age in relative obscurity, but left the world a volume of poems called *Steps to the Temple* that have earned him a prominent place among the seventeenth-century devotional poets in the English canon of literature.

One of my favorite poems of Herbert comes near the very end of his collection, and is entitled simply "Love III" (because he has already written "Love I" and "Love II"). The poem reverses the roles in the above circumstance of the centurion and Jesus in a most shocking way. A sinner is still the distressed one in great need, and Jesus is still the willing healer, but in this poem George Herbert depicts Jesus ("Love") as a tavern hostess! And he depicts himself ("I") as the wayward guest unworthy to be seated for a meal.

When we enter a restaurant or diner today, an attentive host or hostess usually welcomes us with "Can I help you?" or "Would you like to be seated?" In England during Herbert's day (and even still in certain parts of the British Isles), the hostess greeted patrons with "What d' ya lack?" Or, in other words: "What might we provide for you in the way of drink or food or comfort?"

This everyday circumstance results, with the skillful writing and reflective imagination of Holy Mr. Herbert, in a brief and profound exchange by which the poet is beckoned to the eucharistic table.

If you are feeling the need for such a welcome, place yourself at the door of your favorite café and imagine Christ's invitation:

Love III

Love bade me welcome. Yet my soul drew back,
    Guilty of dust and sin.
But quick-eyed love, observing me grow slack
    From my first entrance in,
Drew nearer to me, sweetly questioning,
    If I lacked anything.

A guest, I answered, worthy to be here:
    Love said, You shall be he.
I the unkind, ungrateful? Ah my dear,
    I cannot look on thee.
Love took my hand, and smiling did reply,
    Who made the eyes but I?

Truth Lord, but I have marred them: Let my shame
    Go where it doth deserve.
And know you not, says Love, who bore the blame?
    My dear, then I will serve.

> You must sit down, says Love, and taste my meat:
> So I did sit and eat.[3]

As with every one of us, I suspect, the reluctant customer's excuses for refusing Christ's hospitality are many: I'm guilty of dust and sin. I'm unkind. I'm ungrateful. I have used my eyes and other senses for shameful things. I have marred the gifts that have been given to me. I'm undeserving. I came in by mistake.

Love's insistent hospitality deflects each excuse, not in order to win an argument, but because Love is Love. And Love longs to welcome the guest. "Who?" the Creator asks "made the eyes but I?"—"And know you not," says the one who suffered on the cross, "who bore the blame?"

The speaker's reaction mirrors that of Peter at the Last Supper, who, seeing Christ's sacrificial love, insists on washing Jesus' feet. The gentle insistence of Jesus to Peter is likewise reflected by the host in this poem: "You must sit down and taste my meat." That final word jolts us and we may even suspect that Herbert used it just because he needed a word that rhymed with "eat." Why not bread after all? Well, for one thing we would be expecting bread, and part of the job of poetry is to surprise us. "Meat" stays true to the tavern metaphor that the poet has set up and also communicates in a fresh way what it means to take in the substance of Christ.

In Matthew's gospel the Roman centurion is held up by Jesus as an example of great faith, and his servant is healed within that hour without Jesus ever entering under the man's roof. We, who ritually invite Jesus under our own roofs, know, if we take the time to really consider it, what very unworthy hosts we are. We are equally unworthy guests at Christ's banquet table, of course, and George Herbert reminds us that this is the very point. We are not welcomed to enter into communion with God because we are deserving. Quite the opposite.

"What d' ya lack?" Name it. Faith? Our lack of faith, our guilt and ingratitude have left us hungry and in need of being fed. Love? Love—simple, unconditional, forgiving, welcoming, and healing—insists that we sit with him and eat. This is the communion we crave and the communion God longs to share with us.

"Can I help you?" The reflexive response of most of us is usually "No, I'm good" or "I'm all set." The next time Love beckons—under our unworthy roof or under his—may our response instead be this emphatic prayer: "Yes, yes, yes, Lord! Where shall I sit?"

Part VI

Let the Day Come In

A Prayer in Spring

Robert Frost (1878–1963)

For many people just hearing the name Robert Frost evokes childhood memories of hearing poetry for the first time: "woods lovely, dark, and deep" beneath "downy flake" on "the darkest evening of the year."[1] People quickly conjure two roads diverging in a yellow wood, birches bent over from boys swinging them, abandoned woodpiles, skittish woodchucks and birds, and of course those emblematic New England stone walls in need of repair.

Frostian adages likewise surface to people's minds, woodsy wisdom rendered forth by the white-haired, New England sage: "Good fences make good neighbors," "Something there is that doesn't love a wall,"[2] "Earth's the right place for love,"[3] "I took the [road] less traveled,"[4] "Nothing gold can stay,"[5] "Men work together . . . whether they work together or apart."[6]

As a resident of New Hampshire for more than three decades now, I have grown accustomed to the luxury of having Robert Frost as my most proximate literary neighbor, and you should know if you don't already, that beneath my neighbor's persona of a whimsical pastoral sage repairing his walls and picking apples, resides an individual and artist of great complexity and abundant contradictions.

Start with the fact that he is one of the world's most famous Yankees though he was named after General Robert E.

Lee and was born in San Francisco where he lived for the first eleven years of his life. As Frost's most insightful biographer Jay Parini observes, "The contradictions of [Frost's] life and work remain stunning . . . a loner who liked company; a poet of isolation who sought a mass audience; a rebel who sought to fit in . . . a family man to the core [who] frequently felt alienated from his wife and children . . . a democrat who hated Franklin Roosevelt, [and] a poet of labor who could not support the New Deal."[7]

Robert Frost's views of religion are no less paradoxical. He once described himself as "Presbyterian, Unitarian, Swedenborgian, Nothing." At the same time he had animated conversations with the Jesuits at Holy Cross College and even once delivered a sermon at a Jewish synagogue. As Parini observes, "Having moved around so many churches in childhood," Frost "deliberately stayed away from most churches later in life; nevertheless his correspondence, conversation, and poems are saturated with religious feeling, with questing after God, with evocations of doubt, with meditations on time and eternity." And in one of the last letters Frost wrote in his late eighties, he asked: "Why will the quidnuncs [gossips] always be hoping for a salvation man will never have from anyone but God? I was just saying today how Christ posed himself the whole problem and died for it. How can we be just in a world that needs mercy and merciful in a world that needs justice?"[8]

Here below I have selected a Frost poem whose title speaks for itself as a suitable expression for both the liturgical and natural season that comes with warmer and longer days. "A Prayer in Spring" offers thanks for the earth as it comes back to life, and the eight rhymed couplets are as psalm-like as any words ever spoken to invoke gratitude for the blessings of this earth. What I appreciate most about this short poem is that it was written during "the Derry years" when Frost was a modest, struggling farmer on the outskirts of Derry, New Hampshire. The year was 1906 and Frost had just been hired to teach at Pinkerton Academy, which offered him a much-needed financial boost and a small audience for his teeming ideas. Though he had always been more attentive to his writing than his farm chores, the idea of becoming a famous poet was at that time still but a distant and improbable dream.

The center of this young teacher's world was his wife Elinor and their four children whom they schooled at home. Frost's role in this home instruction included astronomy and botany and other lessons in the natural world. The Derry years would become for Robert and his family a nostalgic counterpoise to many dark events that befell the family in later years. This poem, unlike later idyllic recollections of the Derry years, springs right out of that time and place. The "us" in the poem is most assuredly the Frost family at the Derry farm in 1906. Its melodic simplicity and beauty have always struck me as the words of a father to his children. May they extend across the years to wherever you find yourself and help you give gratitude for spring, however you may find it.

A Prayer in Spring

Oh, give us pleasure in the flowers today;
And give us not to think so far away
As the uncertain harvest; keep us here
All simply in the springing of the year.

Oh, give us pleasure in the orchard white,
Like nothing else by day, like ghosts by night;
And make us happy in the happy bees,
The swarm dilating round the perfect trees.

And make us happy in the darting bird
That suddenly above the bees is heard,
The meteor that thrusts in with needle bill,
And off a blossom in mid-air stands still.

For this is love and nothing else is love,
The which it is reserved for God above
To sanctify to what far ends He will,
But which it only needs that we fulfill.[9]

There are three graces that we ask of God in the sounds and images that fill these lines. First, we beg for the grace to receive the gifts so evident in the world coming to life around us—"the flowers today"—and to receive them without worrying about the future, "the uncertain harvest" "so far away." In the Lord's Prayer we ask to be protected "from all anxieties." Here we repeat that desire: "Keep us here / All simply in the springing of the year."

The second grace we ask is to truly appreciate the remarkable beauty surrounding us: "the orchard white," "the happy bees . . . dilating round the perfect trees," and "the darting bird,"—a hummingbird that Frost describes as descending like a "meteor" and thrusting its "needle bill" into "a blossom," seeming, as it does so, to "stand still" in "mid-air."

The final and most important grace we ask in this prayer is to recognize that all this beauty springs from the love of God. "For this is love and nothing else is love." It is "for God above" to sanctify these things to whatever ends he chooses. Our role is merely to be fulfilled by responding in astonished gratitude.

"I discovered," Frost once wrote to a close friend, "that do or say my damnedest I can't be other than orthodox in politics, love, and religion: I can't escape salvation."[10] May this simple and beautiful prayer that Frost offered on behalf of his family all those years ago become our own. May our own stubbornness and worry, as with that of my familiar and elusive New Hampshire neighbor, fail to make us escape salvation. May this prayer open our eyes and hearts to God by helping us see in the beautiful gift of his creation that "this is love and nothing else is love."

Bicycling to Heaven

Claire Nicolas White (b. 1925)

By midsummer the heat inside many churches can make formal liturgical ritual somewhat challenging. Layers of winter clothing are shed, impending perspiration impinges upon our piety, and, as in Jesus' day, many human toes protrude from sandals. On especially warm days priests often grant their congregation the reprieve of a brief homily, which results often in the kind of succinct and profound wisdom that only brevity can beget. Ordinary Time, of course, is not ordinary. It is punctuated with such great feasts as Corpus Christi, and the full power and meaning of all of those other seasons and feasts settle upon us. Still, as summer sun streams through the stained glass and inadequate rotating fans blow noisily from the back of churches, things are just a bit, well, less solemn than usual.

Like our church, poetry too can often suffer from too much solemnity. Too many people feel like they are not really qualified to read it, that they must somehow approach it on their knees in the literary sanctuary of a classroom, while a teacher reverently opens up the tabernacle of its secret meanings. This is an unfortunate perception. Poetry is really the woman gossiping on her way into church, the daydreaming altar server, or the old man silently weeping in the back pew. And the more sunny and casual days of Ordinary Time are a perfect time for all of us to relax and just behold the next poem or prayer that passes through our cluttered, worried, and extraordinary lives.

How about a poem that would have us get off of our knees and climb onto a bike? Claire Nicolas White's poem "Bicycling to Heaven" sings with the kind of light summer-day optimism that we should not have to be a child in order to experience and celebrate. Claire Nicolas White is the sister of the accomplished sculptress, Sylvia Nicolas, whose work in stained glass and bronze can be seen in many churches and other venues throughout the world. Both women are descended from generations of Dutch artists, and both of them immigrated to America from the Netherlands several decades ago. Claire graduated from Smith College and has succeeded as a translator, poet, novelist, and biographer, authoring several translations and original books. She has lived most of her life in St. James, Long Island, with her husband and sculptor Robert White.

In the short poem I offer here from Claire's 1998 volume *News From Home*, the poet suspends—and invites her readers to suspend—the inevitable uncertainty and disappointments of our spiritual lives. To forget momentarily the thousands of missteps we have made on the rocky path of the straight and narrow road. To forgive the many trespasses we have suffered from others, and to allow God to forgive us in turn. To choose a bicycle of our favorite color and style and happily take a ride with her to the eternal destination we all long to reach:

Bicycling to Heaven

I shall glide on the road to paradise
on silver wheels glistening between trees
as tall as virtues.

I shall be light and clean
bathing in rectangular green pastures
with beasts anchored there.
The road is straight, no mistake.
And though I have not entered
the castle yet, this fortress
grounded like a cow,
I have been on the road
which is enough, for now.[11]

When we think about the road to heaven we are, more often than not, prompted by preachers and by our own experiences to think of it as a rough and rocky climb, a sort of personal Cavalry of our own, punctuated by inevitable stumbles and falls under the weight of our personal sins and crosses. Or we may fancy ourselves, as I often do, chatting worriedly on the road to Emmaus, walking along completely unaware that our traveling companion is Jesus. Maybe sometimes we are running excitedly down a path with Mary Magdalene to share the news of our risen Lord, only to be met by the skepticism of our fellow disciples. Still other times we may imagine ourselves off of the road altogether, up in a tree with Zacchaeus, just hoping for a break.

But have any of us ever imagined bicycling our way to the kingdom of God? Long stretches of winter in our lives, be it actual winter, or grief, or penance, or just despondency, beg for relief from the kind of resolute joy, faith-filled assurance, and even whimsy that this poem offers. In the small prophetic vision that Claire invites us to share, we do not even need to pedal much. She says that she "will glide on the road to paradise / on silver wheels glistening between trees / as tall as virtues." We should note that the road, though it would seem to require little effort, is lined with trees that seem to represent the kind of virtues necessary to shape such a road, and the poet makes clear to potentially puritanical readers, "The road is straight, no mistake."

This is no mere pleasure cruise, but neither is the cyclist on this road someone who is worried about salvation and sin. Rather she envisions herself as having received the full promise of God's redeeming love and she rejoices not just in the destination to which that leads, but in the journey it affords: "I shall be light and clean / bathing in rectangular green pastures / with beasts anchored there." The cows or sheep anchored in the pastures are going nowhere, and God's kingdom is similarly envisioned as a "castle," a "fortress." And seen with childlike playfulness, "grounded like a cow." It is the sort of welcoming permanence and eternal stability we all long for on our roads, though we have "not entered."

Still, as we glide or pedal along, it is the journey to the kingdom, the very lives we are living, rather than the arrival at our eternal destination, that is celebrated in this poem: "I have been on the road / which is enough, for now."

May your next bicycle ride be a prayerful one. And if your cycling days are over, or the paths around you are still buried in snow, or you just need relief from the sorrows, disappointments, and detours on your way to the kingdom, go ahead and try with Claire's help to make your next prayer a bicycle ride. And may that glide between tall trees and pastures be "enough, for now."

Dear World

Sister Mary Faith Schuster, OSB (1914–2007)

Occasionally a student will ask me how I became interested in studying and teaching literature. Such a question arises from a brave and curious place inside a young person who is still trying to figure out the next steps into what can often be a frightful and perplexing future. I respond by telling such students that I met a woman who changed my life. When I then pick up a picture from my bookcase and hand it to them, they are surprised to find themselves looking at the picture of a nun whose white hair halos the space between her face and a small black veil. A nun whose eyes—even in that fading black and white photograph—are somehow blue and piercing, wise and serene.

These are the eyes I first encountered in Sister Mary Faith Schuster, OSB, when I was a very green eighteen-year-old on an improvised college-search trip from my hometown of Denver, Colorado. I had traveled with a friend to the wooded bluffs of eastern Kansas that rise above the vast and meandering Missouri River, and from which one can see for hundreds of miles. I would spend many important hours looking out at the world from those bluffs. But on that first late-winter visit to Atchison, Kansas, and Benedictine College, I sat in the small tidy office of the chair of the English department, listening to the kind voice that went with those eyes and receiving the first of many lessons I would learn from the woman who would become the most important teacher I have ever had.

"You are so young!" Sister Mary Faith told the two of us. These words are usually spoken with condescension, but from this mysterious, ageless woman with the small black veil they resounded with admiration and wonder, as if we were something remarkable that nature had put in her pathway on one of her many walks. Many of us are far too anxious to fill our students with sage advice, but Sister Faith just wanted us to know what a gift we were. And that was her in essence. Nobody ever encountered her, even in passing, without coming away feeling somehow more special.

That trip to Atchison, Kansas, was somewhat unremarkable except for that short conversation. I was still basically clueless about what a Benedictine was, but that brief encounter persuaded me that I wanted to take the next step in my life under the guidance of this woman whom I would come to regard as close to Wisdom herself as I would ever get. A person is richly blessed who can have one teacher like this in a lifetime. Those of us in the English department at Benedictine College during those years had a generous armful. Benedictine sisters opened up books and minds and the world with such tenderness and reverence that my ambition to be a journalist slid off me like the skin of a snake without me ever noticing.

Among her many gifts, Sister Mary Faith was a prolific and remarkable poet. She didn't really write poems. Rather, they spilled out of her on a daily basis as part of the ongoing conversations she held with God and the world he had created. Her life itself was a poem. Raised in a large and devout German Catholic farming family in Pilot Grove, Missouri, she was one of four in her family who took vows as Benedictines; in fact, her younger sister, Sister Scholastica, taught with her in the English department at Benedictine.

In her poetry, Sister Faith harkened back often to the sights and sounds of the farm in the small town where she was raised; the spiderwebs in the barn, the child's wonder on liturgical feast days, the strength of her father's hands, and the sacred songs in her mother's voice. But it was to Mount St. Scholastica Convent in Atchison that she came as a young student and where, but for her years of graduate study at Saint Louis University and other assignments, she lived out her vocation there as a sister, a teacher, an administrator, and a poet.

In 1935, she described her decision to take vows at St. Scholastica Convent (then several hundred sisters strong) in a short poem called "When I Was One and Twenty":

> My desire is a world that reaches
> From star to star.
> My heart is a hungry place
> Where great distances are.
> And yet my peace somehow
> I have come to learn,
> Is a simple and sheltered place
> Where some candles burn.[12]

Choosing what other poem of Sister Faith's to share with people was more challenging than I had imagined. I enlisted my wife for help and we both kept settling on one and then another, each one as delightful and affirming as the next: the coyote encountered in the dark of early morning who is "very sure that / this Missouri field / is his as mine";[13] Simon, who when he took up Jesus' cross on the way to cavalry, teaches us that "perhaps / all books / could / be pared / down / to that /one / moment / each of us / got picked / from the crowd / for something / menial";[14] exuberant conversations with hope, with stars, with fields and flowers; the joy in "the

Creation's / first thunderous command" when "the apple trees awake and "rabbits stir and squirrels / soar and in the quiet cold / the winter birds . . . remember the face . . ." and "everlasting / arms that gave them love."[15]

I went to bed with a dozen such poems ringing in my head and awoke still undecided about which poem to lift from those bluffs by the Missouri River to readers standing in landscapes and cityscapes everywhere. I began to thumb once more through Sister Faith's book of poems until the pages opened, or maybe were opened providentially by my old teacher, to an obvious choice I had somehow missed. What would Sister Mary Faith want to write to you? Of course, her poem from over a quarter century ago called "Dear World."

In deference to the gifts of my good and great teacher, I will do her the grace of simply offering you this poem without any of the explicative insights that would only smudge her words with overthinking. Sister Faith's brief epistle to the world rises from the page as a summer psalm of effusive gratitude. It is a gift from across the years and miles, from the bluffs and fields of eastern Kansas to wherever you find yourself sitting on what I hope is a warm and eternal summer day where you can exhale these words:

Dear World

Almost paralyzed
with summer,
I watch the days go by.

The katydids are interceding,
birds with castanets and harmonies
are on the wind,
looking with good messages
of summer

for people who may
need them.

Let us be quiet, summer,
So the fields can grow:
Let the day come in.
Winter will hurry
Soon enough,
Autumn will blow along
In wind and dusted rain
on wings of its own song.

Let us watch
the birds and let
our needs go on to Heaven
through the invisible
but ever interceding
intercessors from hidden
glory in the bushes
of the night.[16]

Genesis 1:1

Gary Bouchard (b. 1961)

The author of the poem in this section cannot begin to stand beside the poets in this volume. No Hopkins, Rossetti, Shakespeare, Herbert, or Dickinson; that much is certain! But I can offer, without shattering all bounds of modesty, a poem from a quarter century ago that can bring this unusual collection of meditations to a suitable end, or at least back to its beginning. The title of the poem below brings readers to that very opening verse of the Bible, a verse that expresses a profound and profoundly incomplete thought: "In the beginning when God created the heavens and the earth" (Gen 1:1). This beginning of all beginnings is followed by a description of the earth "without form or shape, with darkness over the abyss and a mighty wind sweeping over the waters" (Gen 1:2). Until God gave his very first command, "Let there be light" (Gen 1:3). The frightful and shapeless chaos immediately began to take shape into something that God acknowledged as good. And his work had just begun. Each subsequent day of creation is marked by the refrain that is the essential temporal measure of our lives: "And there was evening and there was morning, the first day."

Who is this Creator God and what is he up to in his whirling world-making? What kind of genius brings order from chaos? What kind of love shaped our world? And to what purpose? We may derive an imaginative answer to such questions by looking up at the ceiling of the Sistine Chapel and seeing the white-bearded world-maker swirling around in clouds, separating the darkness from light. Or, closer to our own homes, we may ponder the daily acts of creation by which we measure our lives.

We may reflect upon the fact that—day by blessed day— through small and great triumphs, in manageable as well as overwhelming difficulties, somewhere between our deepest worries, our most exuberant joys, and the mere passing of time—we are all creators, that in each of our lives "there is evening and there is morning" and another day.

Nobody understands this daily act of creating more than parents, grandparents, and teachers of all kinds, whose job it is to order the universe for the small or not-so-small persons in their charge. In the poem below, the work of God the Creator is conveyed metaphorically and actually in the loving and unending acts of parents whose job it is to bring order to the world of chaos begotten by the ceaselessly busy hands and feet of a busy toddler.

Genesis 1:1

The earth is trampled under
by two small feet
carrying chaos on wings,
sweeping from place
all that order has placed—
teaching objects to fall.

You catch them
to keep the world
from breaking.

Balancing treasures on top shelves,
Keeping things out of reach,
Then handing them down
a piece at a time—
to hold and turn and see
and remember.

The world—
small and blue in a universe of galaxies
is yet too big to know at once.
It must be rationed
in blocks and buckets,
spoon-fulls and cat-tails,
one leaf, then two, then tree,
wave, then water, then sea,
word by word
and truths small enough to be so.

And there is evening
and there is morning
one day.

When chaos is abed
and all objects steadied,
we must go about
replacing the small samples
and pretend
(since it is our house at which we play)
to know where everything on earth belongs.
We must try to see the world at once
and hold and turn and provide.

Everyone who has ever cared for children understands very
much why the God of Genesis rested on the seventh day.
Creation is divinely exhausting work, and try as we may, we

cannot always keep a child's world from breaking. Though we may try to unveil the world "a piece at a time." in all its remarkable splendor as well as its uncertain chaos, we know we are working well above our pay grade. Do any of us really know "where everything on earth belongs"? Haven't most of us in our exasperation felt like we are trying to organize and bring meaning to an "earth without form or shape" (Gen 1:2)?

As our children's first and lasting teachers we offer explanations, "word by word," knowing as we do so that while our words may suffice to stop the unfiltered barrage of questions pouring out of a child, these words do not begin to explain the many wonders of the universe that the child's mind is beholding for the first time. Textbooks may help one day, but now, and now, and always now, St. Paul's three lessons will more than suffice. For we are not merely bluffing our way toward understanding. We are believing, hoping, and loving our way.

We say prayers and say goodnight and turn off the light in a child's room. We turn to reordering our world. "And there is evening / and there is morning / one day." But we are not the ones with the power to declare, "Let there be light" (Gen 1:3). Little in this world yields or moves at our command. We play at making our house, but our work as creators, honestly understood, engenders humility.

It must have been at the end of such a humbling day that I conceived and wrote "Genesis 1:1" over a quarter century ago. The small child who inspired this poem turns twenty-nine this fall and lives more than halfway across the continent. He and his brother continue to achieve so many good things. And yes, even now they are still quite capable of bringing unexpected chaos into our lives. They are not yet entirely out of the reach of their parents' steadying lessons, but try as we must, and love as we will, none of us knows "where everything on earth belongs."

A time may soon come when the grown hands of the toddler that inspired this poem must hold and turn and provide the pieces of creation for two new small hands that carry chaos and spill objects from their place. It is the place of each new generation of parents to keep the world from breaking. As our children learn to create, may they, and may we all, understand that the book of Genesis is a love story; that every breath of the creation story is filled with the love from which it springs and the gratitude it must inspire. May we recognize who ultimately holds, and turns, and provides, and give glory for God's many dappled, striped, and ordinary things.

And there is evening and there is morning, one day.

Amen.

Acknowledgments

"'Hope' is the thing with feathers" J 254/F 314 from THE POEMS OF EMILY DICKINSON, edited by Thomas H. Johnson, Cambridge, Mass.: The Belknap Press of Harvard University Press, Copyright © 1951, 1955, 1979, 1983 by the President and Fellows of Harvard College.

"September, the First Day of School" from *Gnomes and Occasions*, University of Chicago Press, 1973. Reprinted with permission of the author's son, Alexander Nemerov, who acknowledges that the poem is about him.

"Hope" by Kevin Hadduck from *Hymnody of the Blue Heron* published by Cherry Grove Collections, Cincinnati, Ohio, 2016. Reprinted with permission from the author.

"The Song Opens" by Pope John Paul II from *Karol Wojtyla: Collected Poems*, translated with an introductory essay and notes by Jerzy Peterkiewicz, © Liberia Editrice Vaticana. Reprinted with permission.

"Stray Moments" by William Stafford from *Even in Quiet Places*. Copyright © 1996 by The Estate of William Stafford. Reprinted with the permission of The Permissions Company, Inc., on behalf of Confluence Press, www.confluencepress.com.

Notes

I. *When Yellow Leaves or None or Few*

1. Gerard Manley Hopkins, "Pied Beauty," in *Gerard Manley Hopkins*, ed. Catherine Phillips (Oxford: Oxford University Press, 1986), 132–33.

2. Howard Nemerov, "September, the First Day of School," in *The Collected Poems of Howard Nemerov* (Chicago: University of Chicago Press, 1977), 426–27.

3. Shakespeare, "Sonnet 73," in *The Complete Signet Classic Shakespeare* (New York: Harcourt Brace Jovanovich, 1972), 1743.

II. *A Small Thing Always Near*

1. Emily Dickinson, "314," in *The Poems of Emily Dickinson*, ed. R. W. Franklin (Cambridge, MA: The Belknap Press of Harvard University Press, 1999), 116.

2. Kevin Hadduck, "Hope," in *Hymnody of the Blue Heron* (Cincinnati, OH: Cherry Grove Collections, 2016), 79.

3. There is a reproduction of this poem in William Stafford's own handwriting opposite the inside title of his posthumously published book, *The Way It Is: New and Selected Poems* (Minneapolis: Graywolf Press, 1999).

4. William Stafford, "Stray Moments," in *Even in Quiet Places: Poems* (Lewiston, ID: Confluence Press, 1996), 5.

5. Gerard Manley Hopkins, "God's Grandeur," in *Gerard Manley Hopkins*, ed. Catherine Phillips (Oxford: Oxford University Press, 1986), 128.

6. United States Conference of Catholic Bishops, *Magnificat*, in *Catholic Household Blessings and Prayers* (Washington, DC: USCCB, 2007), 41.

7. Pope John Paul II, "The Song Opens," in *Karol Wojtyla: Collected Poems*, trans. Jerzy Peterkiewicz (New York: Random House, 1982), 49.

III. *Gift to this Gift*

1. Christina Rossetti, "A Christmas Carol," in *The Complete Poems of Christina Rossetti*, ed. R. W. Crump (Baton Rouge: Louisiana State University Press, 1995), 215–17.

2. Robert Southwell, "The Nativity of Christ," in *Collected Poems*, ed. Peter Davidson and Anne Sweeney (Manchester: Carcanet Press, 2007), 6.

3. Dana Gioia, "New Year's," in *Interrogations at Noon* (Minneapolis: Graywolf Press, 2001), 16.

4. Alfred Tennyson, "Section 106," *In Memoriam*, in *Tennyson's Poetry*, ed. Robert W. Hill (New York: W. W. Norton, 1971), 178–79.

IV. *To Earth and Ashes*

1. John Donne, "Sonnet 4, O My Black Soul," in *The Complete Poetry and Selected Prose of John Donne*, ed. Charles M. Coffin (New York: Modern Library, 1994), 248.

2. Kilian McDonnell, *Yahweh's Other Shoe* (Collegeville, MN: Saint John's University Press, 2006), 113.

3. McDonnell, "Hogs and Salvation," in *Yahweh's Other Shoe*, 38–39.

4. Dana Gioia, in discussion with the author, June 21, 2007.

5. Gioia, "Litany," in *Interrogations at Noon* (Minneapolis: Graywolf Press, 2001), 10.

6. Melissa Range, "The Conversion of Saul Imagined as a Scene in a Western," in *Horse and Rider* (Lubbock, TX: Texas Tech University Press, 2010), 52.

7. Range, "All Creation Wept," in *Scriptorium* (Boston: Beacon Press, 2016), 55–56.

V. *To Carry Him With Us*

1. Rowan Williams, "Emmaus: Christ Between," in *I Have Called You Friends: Reflections on Reconciliation in Honor of Frank T. Griswold* (Cambridge, MA: Cowley Publications, 2006), 19–20.

2. Denise Levertov, "St. Peter and the Angel," in *Oblique Prayers* (New York: New Directions Publishing, 1984), 79.

3. George Herbert, "Love III," in *The English Poems of George Herbert*, ed. C. A. Patrides (London: J. M. Dent and Sons, 1974), 192.

VI. *Let the Day Come In*

1. Robert Frost, "Stopping By Woods on a Snowy Evening," in *The Poetry of Robert Frost*, ed. Edward Connery Lathem (New York: Holt, Rinehart and Winston, 1969), 224.

2. "Mending Wall," in *The Poetry of Robert Frost*, 33.

3. "Birches," in *The Poetry of Robert Frost*, 121.

4. "The Road Not Taken," in *The Poetry of Robert Frost*, 222.

5. "Nothing Gold Can Stay," in *The Poetry of Robert Frost*, 22.

6. "The Tuft of Flowers," in *The Poetry of Robert Frost*, 22–23.

7. Jay Parini, *Robert Frost: A Life* (New York: Henry Holt, 1999), 446–47.

8. Parini, *Robert Frost: A Life*, 15.

9. Frost, "A Prayer in Spring," in *The Poetry of Robert Frost*, 12.

10. Parini, *Robert Frost: A Life*, 443.

11. Claire Nicolas White, "Bicycling to Heaven," in *News from Home* (Northport, NY: Birnham Wood Graphics, 1998), 42.

12. Mary Faith Schuster, "When I Was One and Twenty," in *Give No End of Praise* (Atchison, KS: Mount Community Center, 1993), 110.

13. Schuster, "The Coyote," in *Give No End of Praise*, 54.

14. Schuster, "Something Menial," in *Give No End of Praise*, 91.

15. Schuster, "All Over Heaven," in *Give No End of Praise*, 19.

16. Schuster, "Dear World," in *Give No End of Praise*, 110.